When I Want
Your Opinion
I'll Tell It To You

The logic, love and laughter that comes from family.

By Vincent F. Orza, Jr.

Table of Contents

Growing Up Can Make You Old

"Learn from the mistakes of others. You won't live long enough to make them all yourself."

I grew up at a time when life in America was wonderful. The 50's were a period of peace, prosperity and calmness. Kids of my generation saw the world through the rose colored glasses of *"Ozzie & Harriet"*, *"Leave It To Beaver"*, *"Father Knows Best"*, *"Make Room for Daddy"* and many other warm, wholesome television shows that gave us the hope of a similar good life.

What TV didn't have was raw violence, vulgarity, and rude parents and children. In the 50's, TV projected innocence, happy endings and the goodness of mankind. Every family had a beautiful, well-dressed perfect housekeeping Mom, a well-dressed patient but stern and understanding Dad. They lived in a wonderful home in the suburbs and enjoyed life.

This contrasts dramatically with what TV, movies and parents show their kids today. The lessons taught to kids by *"MTV"*, *"Roseanne"*, *"Melrose Place"* and the parents that let them watch must be part of the reason today's life in America is so violent, cynical and rude.

Common sense should tell us we are all a product of our environment. Drama of the 50's was mild compared to today. Guns were fired at bad guys but without the blood and guts so common today. Arguments then were resolved in a civil fashion with a happy ending, unlike today's all too common stories of vicious revenge.

Kids were allowed to be children in the fifties. Growing up took more time. Today's kids are bombarded with events, movies, television programs and music that force them to try to be adults before they are ready. Neither their minds nor bodies are ready for much of what they experience. What's worse, the traditional family is in decline and there are fewer positive family role models for kids to pattern their lives after.

Wisdom and maturity come with age and experience. Unfortunately, for many kids today, experience can come without age or even the guidance and wisdom of strong families. It seems that all too many of today's kids are growing up bitter, vicious, vengeful and without a base of family from whom they can gain wisdom.

Perhaps life in the 50's was so much more innocent because kids were more likely to have mothers and fathers to guide them. Dad worked one job and got home at a decent hour. Mom usually didn't work, was waiting for the kids to come home from school and had dinner waiting for the entire family. Dinner, by the way, was eaten without the TV on. Families talked to each other about the day's events, issues in the news and each other. There were more newspapers, magazines and books in our 1950's homes. People read more and had a better knowledge of issues versus knowledge of headlines in today's society.

As quiet as life was, we all knew our lives were part of the bigger world picture. People interacted more in the 50's. If you wanted to chat, you did so with a person not a computer.

Life was better in the 50's because people were nicer, more patient and more accepting. We had our problems and shortcomings in the 50's. Segregation, the KKK and the worry of a communist infiltration could have destroyed our democracy.

I believe we survived these threats because Americans were more tolerant of each other...better read, more accepting of our immigrant heritage, open to change and committed to freedom for everyone. America and its' people lived a better life in the 50's. Sadly, many in my generation didn't learn the lessons of their parents and grandparents. Today's America talks family values better than they practice them. Families don't eat together at dinner with or without TV. Families don't read as much or as many things as they did in the 50's.

Family entertainment today doesn't build togetherness as well as Donna Reed, Red Skelton, and Ed Sullivan did in the 50's. Perhaps most of all, America today lacks the warm, friendly sense of humor that helped it recover from the dark days of the Depression, World War II and nuclear threat of the 50's.

Until recently, America was always good at laughing at itself, its people, and its religious and ethnical diversity. What follows is an attempt to bring a little humor back from growing up in the 50's. All of it is a reflection of growing up in a more innocent time; a time that helped America and all of its' people live a better life.

Don't get me wrong; families of years past had their problems as well. Divorce, abuse and violence are not new but they do seem to be more prevalent. One thing is for sure; we laughed more in years past. We laughed innocently at each other and ourselves. Our jokes and stories were meant to be harmless rather than critical. The jokes and stories we heard on the Ed Sullivan Show by Milton Berle, Myron Cohen, Dean Martin and Jerry Lewis, and Abbot and Costello never drew blood. Movies and books were descriptive, but allowed us to use our imagination. Today, "talk radio" is vicious, critical, and almost uncontrolled. From Howard Stern to Rush Limbaugh, search and destroy radio is cut throat. Books and movies are sold on action and skin rather than by acting or plots. Perhaps it's time for a look back to more tranquil times.

Hopefully my observations of life as a kid will help today's America relax and laugh a little more. It's time to lighten up on ourselves and regain the strength of America's diversity and sense of humor. It's what made us become the world's only super power.

I hope my warm memories help you remember some of yours.

"To be able to enjoy one's past life is to live twice."
Martial (A.D. 86)
Epigram x.23,7

1 Immigrant Logic

"When you come to a fork in the road, take it."
"Whatever you do in life, 90% of it is half-mental."

- Yogi Berra

I have some terrific memories from growing up in Connecticut in the 1950's. We were a family of first and second-generation immigrants. Virtually all of my immediate family was born in New York City. The ethnic groups that inhabited it defined each street. By the time I came along my folks had ventured across the border into Connecticut. Ten years before I was born, my folks bought a very small bungalow just off the beach, and added enough rooms to more than double the size of the house. Pop and the neighbors did all of the work. I came from the ideal American dream family with a father who worked long and hard and a June Cleaver mom.

Our home was a terrific little place that our entire New York family of uncles, aunts, cousins and grandparents visited often. To a stranger, having that much family around would be a nightmare. To my family, more family was important; it was a topic of conversation that could never be depleted.

Sunday dinners were big family events; ten or fifteen people were common. When more people came than we could seat at the dining room table, we took the bedroom doors off their hinges and laid them over chairs to increase the seating with a large piece of plywood on the table for additional dining space. Dinners lasted for hours, with stories of the war, the kids, and the trips from Italy and holidays gone by.

We're Italians. We eat for any and every reason. There isn't an event or holiday that can't be turned into a feast. Eating meant talking and listening to the old people reminisce. Italians respect age. "Listen to the old man," "Ask Grandma," "What does Uncle Eddie think?" Children should be seen and not heard was a common expression, yet the kids were always included in the conversation if for no other reason than to sit, listen and learn. When it came to the kids' opinions, the standing joke in our family was *"When I want your opinion, I'll tell it to you."*

Back to eating. The order of the day was to eat. Clean your plate. We weren't permitted to not like something. If I didn't eat everything on my plate, my mother would advise me: "There are people starving in China." If we didn't like what was being served we were asked: "What do you think this is, a restaurant?" My mom was and is a terrific cook. Our house always had enough food so ten extra people could stop in and join us for dinner on the spur of the moment. Neighbors and family would say, "Eda, we don't want to impose," but they did without any guilt or hesitation. Neighbors dropped in around dinnertime and sat down to a host of dishes they couldn't identify but looked, smelled and tasted terrific. They ate everything. Mom explained to us "beggars can't be choosers." As much as Mom complained about the constant flow of unannounced guests, she loved to cook for them.

If you want to insult my mom, tell her you're not hungry, don't eat or even worse, eat only a little bit.

Mom: "Eat!"

Neighbor: "I did."

Mom: "You eat like a bird."

Neighbor: "Really, I'm full. It was wonderful."

Mom: "What's the matter? You didn't like it?"

Neighbor: "No, it was great."

Mom: "If it was so great, why didn't you eat more?"

It went on like this every meal, everyday. My mom doesn't believe you can eat too much. My mom also hates waste. If we went on a picnic, we brought real plates.

Mom: "What paper plates, they're a waste of money. Bring real plates, whatsa matter, aren't you coming home?"

Vincent: "Yeah, of course."

Mom: "So, you'll bring the plates home. Why waste money on paper plates?"

We never, (and still don't) discard empty jars, bottles or containers that can be re-used. Frugality is part of being an immigrant. I still rinse off aluminum foil and re-use plastic and paper bags. Of all the things people can purchase, garbage bags really confused Mom.

Mom:	"What's that?"
Neighbor:	"What?"
Mom:	"That in that box?"
Neighbor:	"A box of garbage bags."
Mom:	"You buy garbage bags? Do you buy garbage too?"
Neighbor:	"No of course not."
Mom:	"So why buy bags to put your garbage in. Grocery bags are for garbage. That's why the stores give them to you. Otherwise, you'd take home the groceries in an old box, which by the way you should save to store things in!"

The rule at our house was "No waste." Peanut butter jars held garlic. Every ounce of meat, bone and fat was used to make something from soup to stew. Intestines held sausage, feathers went in pillows, and rags were used to make braided rugs. We never wasted a thing.

Rule #1: **Don't buy something new until something old is worthless.**

Rule #2: **Nothing is worthless. You may not want it but someone else might.**

Rule #3: **Don't throw anything away. Find someone who wants it. If someone wants it, it must have some value, so maybe you shouldn't give it away.**

"What could they know about this that I don't? I better keep it until we find out why they want it."

Old large sheets (before they had fitted corners) were cut down to small sheets for baby cribs. Baby sheets were used as rags.

"Who needs paper towels? I've got real towels and rags. Why pay money for something you use once and throw away? Wash and dry that Saran Wrap. Why throw it away when it still works?"

On the special occasions that we did eat out, Mom told us: "Get a doggy bag. If the dog doesn't eat it, we will. After all, we ordered it in the first place. Besides, we could use the bag for your sandwich at lunch."

And when we did eat out Mom always said the same thing no matter what we ate.

"It was good, not as good as I make, but it was ok."

Hotels are always a treat for my family. Not only do you get a nice place to sleep but you can grocery shop as well. You see my family believes if you pay for a hotel, you should use it. I mean everything. Hence, no one in the Orza family has purchased a bar of soap since 1953. You can look in our bathroom cabinets and find enough hotel soap to sink a ship. When we checked in, we instantly collected the extra soap and put it in our luggage. We even ask the maids for extra soap. We also had a pretty decent supply of shampoo, conditioner, mouthwash, sewing kits and stationery! We paid for it didn't we?

Have you ever gotten those free offers in the mail to go look at real estate? Most people think these offers are a waste of time and effort. Most people aren't Orza's. My folks would (and did) drive half way across the continent for $100 bucks and a free weekend stay for seeing a vacation condominium in Arkansas.

Vince: "Pop, why go all the way to see a condo you don't want to buy?"

Pop: "I'm not going to see the condo, I'm going to see the $100 bucks.

I'm no better. I received an offer in the mail for a free coffeepot if I'd join a coffee of the month club. No obligation, I buy one pound of coffee a month and if I don't like it, I keep the coffeepot. End of discussion. My wife tries to explain to me that we don't need a coffeepot. I try to explain to her what my parents have explained to me. "How could you not need a free coffee pot?" Someone we know will get a great coffeepot from us for Christmas!

We are also avid readers. Hence we joined the Book of the Month Club. After all, you get the first 10 books for just $1. Then over the next two years you have to purchase four additional books. The average price for a book is $15, times 4 is $60 total. For $60 bucks you got 14 books...for a real average price of

$4.28. NO WASTE and someone we know will get a nice book for Christmas!

We were the normal church-going family. Which is to say we went to church most Sundays. As a little kid, I thought I had church figured out. Got up early, got dressed fancy, went to church, sat still (very difficult to do without getting in trouble), stood up, sat down, stood up, kneeled, stood up, gave money, got a tiny piece of bread from some big shot guy up front who had hundreds of children. I know this because everyone called him "Father"!

One day I decided to go to mass on my own. At the ripe old age of about four, I put on my bathing suit, got one penny from my piggy bank and walked about one mile to church. When my parents realized I was missing, near pandemonium broke out as they searched everywhere for me, never, of course, thinking I'd gone to church.

The priest that found me called my folks to let them know I was safe. Pop and Mom came to get me and found me sulking and mad. Somehow I had decided the Priest wouldn't let me in because I didn't have enough money. To me, one penny was a fair price for such a small piece of bread!

"Common sense is genius dressed in its working clothes."
- Ralph Waldo Emerson

2 Holidays Are The Reason God Created Food

"After a good dinner, one can forgive anybody, even one's own relatives."

- Oscar Wilde

For Italians, holidays are another excuse to eat. Every Sunday and every holiday we had macaroni. The only difference on holidays was that we had the holiday special food after the macaroni. It's Easter, "We'll have macaroni and I'll roast a lamb. It's Thanksgiving we'll have macaroni & I'll make a turkey," It's the 4th of July. "We'll make some macaroni and eat at the beach like a picnic with some chicken, roast beef, and beer." The beer made it a picnic for Italians; otherwise we would have had wine. The wine, beer and liquor were also for the kids.

"How they gonna learn to drink if they don't learn to drink?" (More immigrant logic).

"Vincent, don't gulp. Wine is made to be sipped."

Wine for the kids was cut with cream soda and offered with every dinner.

"Pop, can I have a sip of your wine?"

My father's response was always a silent nod of the head signifying yes. He'd offer the glass or bottle. Only if the sip was too long did he admonish me.

"Don't be a wise guy, drink right, Mr. Big Shot."

We learned to drink responsibly but rarely without food. NO ONE ever got drunk.

The Easter lamb, by the way was a whole lamb, head and all. Every year my father would bribe me. "I'll give you a dollar if you eat the eye." I never got the dollar. The feast of Easter related to the Lamb of God. The fact is every holiday had its ritualistic food; almost always for religious reasons.

Christmas was best of all. Catholics were supposed to fast on Christmas Eve. No meat. Somehow Italians convinced the church that fish was a sacrifice for God and the birth of Christ." We had clams, mussels, shrimp, baked fish, broiled fish, raw fish, fish with spaghetti and lobster.

More immigrant logic...lobster is a sacrifice!

Americans have turkey on Thanksgiving. Italians do too, along with the antipasto, soup, lasagna, maybe a small roast beef, fruit, nuts, dessert, wine (red and white...don't forget we had the roast beef and turkey) and a few dozen liqueurs to finish up after the coffee (regular and espresso). Italian Americans loved the pilgrims because there wasn't a good Italian or Catholic holiday in November. Thanksgiving gave us a reason to celebrate in November!

By the way, the first day back at school after a holiday always made Italian kids popular.

Friend: "Yo, Vinny, what do you got for lunch?"

Vinny: "Nothin' special."

Friend: "What's in the thermos?"

Vinny: "Soup."

Friend: "What's that?"

Vinny: "Just some chicken, I think it's a drumstick."

Friend: "What's that?'

Vinny: "A veal cutlet sandwich."

Friend: "What's in the jar?"

Vinny: "A few roasted peppers."

Friend: "What, no dessert?"

Vinny: "Just cheesecake and some fruit."

Immigrant logic. You can't learn if you are hungry.

Only now do I realize what the teachers must have had to endure with a room full of kids, whose stomachs contained some of the world's most powerful foods. I was 16 when I finally realized why all the Italian, Cuban, Spanish and Greek kids were made to sit next to the window and why the windows were always open, even in the dead of winter! In a good ethnic neighborhood, dinnertime could produce enough natural gas to heat all of South Dakota!

Because food is such a central part of life to Italians, you'd think we eat in restaurants all the time. Not my family.

> Mom: "What do you mean eat out? Whatsa matter, you don't like my cooking?"

Immigrant logic. Taking Mom out to dinner at a restaurant was an insult. Bringing a friend home to dinner; a compliment!

I'm in the restaurant business but I still prefer to cook and eat at home rather than in a restaurant. I was 38 years old before I had my first and only piece of Kentucky Fried Chicken. Fast food can't be Italian. Why eat fast? Who eats in the car? Italians aren't in a rush to eat…considering how fast they drive; it's a good thing. When we do eat in restaurants, we want to eat well. Veal chops, lamb chops, pasta (the 1980's and 90's word for macaroni or spaghetti), and fresh fish. We want a drink or bottle of wine with a salad (after dinner, not before).

Americans have their salad before dinner and fill up on lettuce. Europeans understand salad is cheap; meat is expensive. Eat as much meat as possible (no waste) and then finish up with salad (which, by the way, is almost always dressed with oil and vinegar, which also helps you digest your meal).

Immigrant logic. The sooner you digest a meal, the sooner you can eat again!

"Life is short, live it up."
- Nikita Khrushchev

3 Holiday Traditions

"You're only young once. After that it takes some other excuse for behaving like an idiot."

- Will Rogers

Halloween today is a business. Today, kids need flash lights, reflectors, and parents driving in cars, police escorts and armed guards. When I was a kid, trick or treating was more fun and it was safe. Kids today are missing the Halloween boat. They go to the store, buy some lousy $10 or $20 costume, and use a lousy brown paper bag full of advertising for their loot. My mom made my Halloween costumes. I was a Hobo, a girl, a gypsy, a pirate and a clown. We never bought a plastic pumpkin or fancy bag for our candy. I used a pillowcase. It was big, strong and could be a weapon for self-defense if a bigger kid tried to steal your candy.

Sometimes I was two or three things in one night, especially for the old lady three blocks over. Most people gave homemade candy, candied apples, popcorn balls, cake, a piece of pie, fresh baked brownies, fresh apple cider (Connecticut is apple country) and apples. But the old lady three blocks over gave cold hard cash.

We'd go to her door hollering trick or treat and she'd hand each of us a quarter. It may not sound like much today but it was a bonanza in 1957. You got an apple or candy bar from everyone else, both worth a nickel. The old lady's quarter was like visiting five houses, and worth running all the way home to change costumes for two or three other collections. I'd still run home for the quarter and yes, I do pick up pennies on the street, although, usually my daughters spot them first. My wife made our girls' Halloween costumes, and I told them to remember the houses with the best treats. My grandfather always said, "The apple doesn't fall too far from the tree." Immigrant logic.

Holidays have changed over the years. When I was a kid, we spent every major holiday with all my uncles, aunts, cousins and grandparents. At Christmas, we'd load up the car with "a" gift for everyone who would be at dinner.

Families today are too spread out. It's become the exception rather than the rule when uncles, aunts, cousins and grandparents spend a holiday together. When I was a kid, there were no nursing homes. No matter how old or sick Grandma and Grandpa were, they lived with or next door to you. Today they live in Florida by themselves and you give them a call to wish them Merry Christmas before the family sits down to a frozen or store bought dinner.

We opened our presents on Christmas morning. It didn't take long. Everybody got one thing and occasionally Pop got a gift for the house. This would be the new "hi fidelity stereo", color television or pots and pans for Mom.

When Patti and I married, I saw a whole new approach to Christmas. Her family came together to exchange gifts...as though there would never be another Christmas. There were hundreds of presents to be shared by a handful of people and they were opened on Christmas Eve. It took hours to unwrap the gifts because one person would unwrap a gift while everyone else watched. Then another person would unwrap a gift while everyone watched him. It went on for hours. While it seemed gluttonous to me, I grew to like it when I realized I was getting a department store full of gifts as well.

When I was a kid, I hated to go to sleep on Christmas Eve, yet I knew I had to if Santa was going to come. I still remember the time I sneaked back out only to find Pop putting my Santa gift under the tree. Christmas morning I opened "Santa's" gift knowing Santa lived much closer than the North Pole.

Christmas for Patti, the girls and me took on Patti's family tradition. We opened almost everything Christmas Eve. First of all Santa would stop by our house while we were opening the gifts. Every Christmas Eve, just as we were about to start unwrapping, I would get a call to run to the office for an emergency. While I was gone, lo and behold, Santa would stop by, say hello to our girls, and give them two "small" presents he wasn't going to be able to fit on his sleigh on the real trip later that night. For years my girls never recognized me, or in later years friends, as Santa. They always felt special knowing that with millions of kids to visit, Santa would make an extra trip to our house.

Indeed, before I left on my emergency call, I would stand in the doorway with the girls and we would watch for Santa's sleigh and reindeer. I would point up to the sky and sure enough, the girls would see and hear the sleigh bells and reindeer. After hours of opening our family presents on Christmas Eve, everyone would go to bed. The next morning there were still more gifts for the girls left by Santa while we all slept.

When I was a kid, Christmas was the only holiday I got presents. Other than a chocolate bunny at Easter, Christmas was it. Patti believes every holiday is Christmas. My girls not only got chocolate bunnies at Easter, but another load of Easter presents. Each Easter morning the girls would awake just in time to see the Easter bunny hopping away. It's amazing what kids will see if you just throw a little fertilizer on their imaginations. Left behind at our front door, were baskets of candy, toys, games, clothes and a host of other gifts, including the "Golden Egg" that came complete with a special poem written by the Easter Bunny. The poem told them where to look for the extra special Easter gifts! This was all new to me. How the hell did the Easter bunny store all this stuff? I finally realized the Bunny used Santa's sleigh to haul all the loot, or at least that's what I told the girls!

To Patti, every holiday is a reason to give the girls a gift. Thankfully, the girls appreciated what they received and never took it for granted. We also started one other tradition. Every Christmas and birthday I write each of the girls a poem to tell them how much we love them and help remember things that have happened in their lives that year. We have a picture taken of the girls every year and it hangs with their poem on our bedroom wall. We have a gallery of pictures and poems to gaze at each night before we go to sleep. Traditions are for memories and our pictures and poems help us remember each year of the girls' lives.

By the way, our daughter Landi has taken up the art of poetry. Now she also writes them to be included with gifts on special occasions. Good traditions are like poison ivy - they spread!

Immigrants bring many wonderful traditions with them when they come to America. It's sad so many traditions have been forgotten. What's even sadder is that all too many families don't create new ones to take the place of those forgotten. Ethnic or religious symbolism provides reasons for doing things a certain way and make our lives worth living.

Immigrant logic. Enjoy every opportunity to celebrate family and God...anybody's. God speaks all languages and he/she will know what you mean.

"God created man because he was disappointed in the monkey."

- Mark Twain

4 Mind Your Own Damn Business

"Two things in life are certain...death and taxes. But at least death doesn't get worse each time Congress reconvenes."

- Will Rogers

By their nature, immigrants stay among themselves. Language and cultural barriers make it easier to associate with people of like backgrounds. Having said that, immigrants enjoy watching from afar the way other cultures celebrate life. What they don't enjoy is people butting into their lives and life styles.

Italians love only one thing more than food and that's kids. Come to think of it, having kids around leads to food. "I'm pregnant." "Salute. Let's celebrate. Open a bottle of wine; we'll make a toast. I'll make a roast beef, some macaroni, bake a cake and we'll invite everyone over to make the announcement." Or if you brought a kid from school home to play, you'd hear this. "Who'sa this boy?" "Dun cha eat at home?" "Sitta down and I feed you so you not so skinny like a bird."

Passing judgment is something my family was good at. He's too short; he's very tall. He's the fat guy; he's the lush. She's got nice legs and she shows them off too much. Don't be so proud of those nice legs. Oh, she's a cute girl, and look at the big bosom. Look how's she's dressed, she looks like a street walker."

We were also good at giving advice and even better at giving some hell. I'll never forget the time my mother, sister and I were in a grocery store. My sister had her baby son with her. As we were checking out of the store the baby began to cry. A woman in line behind us said something to the effect that my mother and sister were not taking care of the baby..."look the poor child is hungry...why don't you feed him?"

As I said, immigrants don't like outsiders intruding in their personal lives, especially when it comes to kids. The woman behind us wouldn't leave it alone. Finally my mother let her have it with "why don't you mind your own damn business? When I want your opinion, I'll ask for it." Needless to say, the woman never uttered another word.

Years later, I ran for Governor of Oklahoma. The state had real problems with its schools and economy. My campaign was built around my experience in business and education. I felt I knew something about those issues. While I had no experience in politics, my message began to catch on. As the primary election drew closer, the other candidates, who were lawyers, started to change their tune. None had any experience in business or education, but before I knew it they were all claiming to be businessmen. Fortunately, voters were smart enough to know inheriting your father's oil wells or being a bankruptcy lawyer didn't qualify you as a "businessman." So, the lawyers turned to the one issue I avoided.

Abortion was a hot political topic for Republicans in 1990, at least for everyone but me. My doctorate was in education not medicine and I'm a man. Inasmuch as I was never going to be pregnant, didn't come from a medical or religious background, I didn't feel I was qualified to pass judgment on a woman who was pregnant and didn't want to be. While none of the other guys had female, medical or religious credentials either, they all claimed to be "pro-life" candidates. I avoided the issue which instantly made me the "pro-choice" or as the hard liners called me, PRO-ABORTION candidate. To me it was none of my business. I said if I were a woman who was pregnant and didn't want to be, I might discuss it with my doctor, with my priest or minister, with GOD...but I sure wasn't going to call the Republican Party and ask them what to do. I've yet to understand how Republicans can say less government but then want it to intrude on the most personal matter a woman can face.

Well this was pro-choice to the hard liners. One night at dinner I asked my 75-year-old mother what she thought about abortion. "What the hell business is it of yours or any man's what a woman does with her body. You're never going to be pregnant. They should all mind their own damn business." My mother wasn't for abortion; she was for people butting out of each other's private lives. Way to go Mom! General Colin Powell said it best, "God provides us with guidance and inspiration, not a legislative agenda."

During President Clinton's Monica Lewinsky episode, much of America felt compelled to pass judgment. In the old days if someone had an affair, it was between the husband and wife to resolve. The resolution should be made in the best interest of the children, as in they "stayed together for the sake of the kids." If the President and his wife have resolved their problems and in the process raised a terrific daughter, shouldn't they get credit for that?

Americans today seem to have a problem minding their own business. All America learned about the nation's first woman B-52 pilot committing adultery. Then we learned an Air Force General slated to be the next Chairman of the Joint Chiefs had an affair 13 years ago. It seems America is not being very adult about adultery. Issues like abortion and adultery are private and religious, not political. Biblically we are advised to "let he who is without sin cast the first stone." Or as Mom says, "MIND YOUR OWN DAMN BUSINESS!

"There is no vice like advice."

- Mark Twain

5 What Are You, Helpless?

"You have to keep busy. Dogs never pee on a moving car."

- Tom Waits

My mother kept a spotless house. If you were eating soup and paused for a moment, she eyed your dish as something to clean. We vacuumed the rug daily, even though no one was allowed in the living room unless we had company.

Rule #4: **Family is not company. Only strangers are company but they're nice people. We'll treat them like family. So stay out of the living room.**

I swear my mother could wear out a brand new carpet by vacuuming it.

When families came together we always stayed in the kitchen and dining room. Why should we go in the living room? "Who we gonna impress. They've been here before. The first time they're a guest...after that they're a pest. Sit down at the table...here, eat something, you look skinny."

I was taught to make my bed under threat of death. It was clear, never leave your bed unmade, no dirty dishes in the sink, flush the toilet (and for God sakes, put the seat down).

"Clean up after yourself, young man. What do you think this is a hotel? There's no maid here. I'm the maid, and I'm no maid." (More immigrant logic.)

Cleanliness was not only next to Godliness; it was next to impossible to be too clean.

"Brush your teeth."

"Comb your hair."

"Did you wash behind your ears?"

"Are your nails clean?"

"Do you have on clean underwear?"

"Bring home the plastic bag your sandwich was wrapped in and I'll wash it out and we'll use it again tomorrow."

This was the bag we bought fruit in from the grocery store or the doggy bag from the restaurant.

"What do you think we're made of, money? Do you think money grows on trees?"

By the way, invariably every one of the clichés ended up with a warning of things to come.

"You'll see, some day you'll have kids. I hope your kids do to you what you did to me." (I call this the "Curse of Mommy.")

When I was a kid and I would stub my toe or bruise my leg, Mom would say "That's God punishing you!" "For what?" I'd say. Mom's reply was simple. "I don't have to know. God knows!"

My parents never gave me an allowance.

Pop: "Allowance, what I gotta pay you to live here? You don't have to live here. You want me to help you pack your bags? Allowance...your allowance is I allow you to live. That's your allowance. You're lucky I don't make you pay to live here."

My father always told us "If you want something, ask for it."

Pop: "Besides, what could you want? Your mother and I give you everything. When I was a boy, I didn't have my own bedroom much less my own bed. I shared the bed with your two uncles. So maybe you want money for food? You don't need money for food. Your mother makes you a lunch for school. You eat better than the principal."

Vincent: "Pop, my bike's too small for me. Can I get a new bigger bike?"

Pop: "Why a new bike, a bigger bike? Is a new, bigger bike gonna get you there sooner? I didn't have a bike when I as a kid. I rode the subways."

Vincent: "Pop, you grew up in New York, they had subways. We don't have subways in Connecticut."

Pop: "What's that got to do with you needing a new bike? I didn't get a new subway as I got older."

Vincent: "Never mind, Pop."

My folks are great savers. I'd guess they saved 50 cents out of every dollar they had. Pop has yet to buy a car without paying cash. They taught all of us to save.

Mom: "Come on, we're going to the bank today. We've got to put $2 in our Christmas club account."

Rule #5: Always save something from everything you earn. Never borrow money unless it's for a house. (Because a house is for family.)

Later on as car prices rose, Pop gave in and told us we could buy both a house and car on time...but nothing else — (cars for no more than three years). Pop thinks drive-in banks were created so cars could see their real owners. He, of course, never bought a car on time.

Pop: "To get a loan you gotta answer too many questions. It's none of their business. Sign this - sign that. If I give my word, then I'll pay it back. I don't need to sign anything. Why do they need to know how much I make, how much I saved, if I went to school, and my social security number? Prisoners of war only tell their name, rank and serial number. Getting a loan shouldn't be worse than being a prisoner of war."

"Alexander Hamilton started the U.S. Treasury with nothing and that's the closest we've ever been to being even."

What Are You, Helpless?

6 Sort Of Liberal

Conservative - is someone who believes nothing
should be done for the first time!

I always thought my father was an Attila the Hun,
archconservative. But as I look back, I now believe he was sort of
liberal. Everybody else's father (at least non-Italians) prohibited
their kids from drinking. At our house, it was S.O.P. (standard
operating procedure), wine with dinner. When it came time to go
out, everyone else's father told them when to be home. My folks
were different. I was never told what time to come home.
Instead, I was asked what time I'd be home.

Vincent: "See you later."

Pop: "Where are you going?"

Vincent: "To the game."

Pop: "How you getting there?"

Vincent: "Tim's folks are driving."

Pop: "Tim, the Irish kid? His father's a lush, be
careful. Sit in the back seat so if he crashes
into a wall you won't get killed. What time
you coming home?"

Vincent: "Midnight."

At that moment, I had single-handily put a noose around my
neck. God help me if I came in three seconds after midnight. My
folks believed in giving me all the rope I needed to hang myself.
If I said midnight, midnight was fine. I set my own rules so I
should be more than willing and able to abide by them. I got
home late only once in my life. Pop was wide-awake and waiting
for me.

Pop: "Come here, Bud. Where you been?"

Vincent: "To the ball game."

Pop: "Did you win?"

Vincent: "Yea!"

Pop: "Did you have fun?"

Vincent: "Yea."

Pop: "What time did you say you 'd be home?"

By this time I knew death was near.

Vincent: "Midnight, Pop."

Pop: "What time is it?"

Pop knew how to always drag out the pain for its maximum effect.

Vincent: "It's...(slow down, Vince, don't act like it's no big deal for Pop to be awake after midnight) a little after midnight."

The word "little" was supposed to make Pop believe I wasn't really late...just delayed. He wasn't buying!

Pop: "Did you say you'd be home a little after midnight?"

Vincent: "No, but..."

Pop: "You're right, no buts."

Vincent: "But..." (Put a lid on it, Vincent, you can't win).

Pop: "You know if you wanted to be home at one minute after midnight or five minutes after midnight or two o'clock, all you had to do was say so."

Vincent: "Yes, sir."

Apparently I was not agonizing enough, so Pop decided to drag out the torture a little further.

Pop: "What time did you say you'd be home?"

Vincent: "Midnight."

Pop: "I didn't hear you. What time?"

About that time my mother walked in. As I look back, I think they rehearsed this routine.

Mom: "Vincent, is that you?

Now the only ones living in that house were Mom, Dad and I, so the question was asked just to induce pain.

Vincent: "Yes, Mom."

Mom: "What time is it?"

My mother must have been a concentration camp officer or prison warden!

Vincent: "It's a little after midnight, Mom."

Mom: "How come you're late? Are you okay? Did something happen? We were worried something might have happened to you."

In other words, is there any reason why I shouldn't let your father kill you for lying to the two people who love you more than life itself? The two people who sat here for hours waiting for you to come home safe and sound, to your own room (with clean sheets) at midnight?

Vincent: "No, Mom, nothing happened. I'm just late."

Mom: "Oh."

Vincent: "I promise it won't happen again."

Then Pop came in for the kill.

Pop: "You bet it won't happen again. If it does you can go live with Tim and his father, the lush."

Gee, that's not too bad. I expected a longer lecture and some punishment.

Pop: "And just in case you don't understand... you're grounded for the rest of the month."

Bull's-eye.
Pop 2 - Vincent 0.
Game - Set - Match.

"Any child can tell you that the sole purpose of a middle name is so he can tell when he's really in trouble."

- Dennis Fakes

7 More Liberal Than I Knew

> "Too many cannot read or write; though they can multiply."
>
> - Art Buck

Like everyone, my family has its prejudices. And like many, we also know what it was like to be discriminated against. Pop has told the story thousands of times about the country club with the sign out front that proudly stated "No Ginnys, Jews, or Dogs Allowed." Those who have been locked out are sympathetic to others facing the same treatment. When I was a kid in New York and Connecticut in very ethnic neighborhoods there were no blacks. The terms Negroes and niggers were used very commonly. For as much as my family hated to be called ginnys, wops and grease balls, it seemed to never occur to them or anyone else that blacks wouldn't appreciate being called niggers. Jews didn't like being called kikes; Irish didn't like the name micks, yet all of us had names reflective of our religion, race or ethnicity. I was Vinny the ginny. I have scars to prove it.

Pop did business with Sam the Jew, Clarence the nigger, Mike the mick and others. These names, by the way, had some affection applied to them and were used to their face as well as behind their backs.

It never occurred to me that my father was any more prejudiced than anyone else was but I did and do believe he certainly is less prejudiced than many. Pop and his brothers had a lot of employees that became friends and one long time employee they treated like family. His name was Clarence Green. Clarence was a wonderful black gentleman who did everything and anything on the job. He called my dad, Mr. Jim, my uncles, Mr. Eddie and Mr. Vic. He called me Mr. Vincent.

During the 50's, black and white relationships were pretty black and white. They were oil and water, yet everyone in our family knew Clarence was a friend, not a black man...just a gentleman who deserved respect, courtesy and friendship. The kids learned lesson number one...color isn't a good reason to hate someone.

Pop also spoke with great reverence for a man named Benny Kaufman. When my father was starting his trucking business, Benny sold him gas. During Pop's first week on the job, he went to pay for the gas. Pop counted out the cash and after payment, had $40 for himself. Benny said, "Is that all you have left?" Pop replied, "Yes." Benny counted out $50 and gave it to my father telling him, "Your wife will need more than $40 to take care of your kids." Benny trusted the upstart dago kid and the upstart dago kid appreciated the old Jew's generosity and concern.

Likewise, when my uncle remarried after the death of his first wife, the family taught the kids the second lesson. Religion isn't a reason to hate someone. My Uncle Eddie was head of our family. Everyone loved him and Aunt Rose. Rose died young and left two children. My cousins Cathy and Eddie became everyone's family. Italians revere mothers and children. To this day, my cousin Ed and I are like twin brothers. We trust and would do anything for each other. We learned that from our fathers who felt the same way about their brothers.

Anyway, Aunt Rose passed away and sometime later Uncle Ed decided to remarry. Goldie became my new aunt. Goldie was/is a Jew. In the 1950's an Italian Catholic marrying a Jew was anything but common. Eddie's decision to marry Goldie was the hot topic of family conversation but it boiled down to one thing. Religion was not an issue when it came to family happiness.

Rule #6:   Religion is good...even someone else's.

My folks passed these lessons of nondiscrimination onto their kids. In 1957 or '58, my sister graduated from high school. I remember one thing about that day. My sister, Connie was decked out in her cap and gown. After the ceremonies were over, she brought one of her best friends over to meet my folks. I don't remember her name (I'm sure Connie does) but I do remember her friend was black. I didn't see too many other white kids with black friends that day.

The message my folks sent us, was that friends (no matter what color) are good. Likewise, my folks never questioned my choice of friends or girl friends. When I started dating a Jewish girl in junior high, my folks' remarks were simple; "She's pretty." I know for a fact that other kids were told they could not date a Jew, a Protestant, or have black kids over to play. As conservatives go, our family was pretty liberal. They were open-minded and trusted their kids to use good judgment. That could be Rule #7 – Use good judgment! If they're nice to you – be nice to them…if they're not nice to you – be bigger than they are…but not a bigger jerk.

"My blackness has been a source of pride, strength and inspiration and so has my being an American. I started out believing in an America where anyone given equal opportunity, can succeed through hard work and faith. I still believe in America."

- General Colin Powell

8 Everybody's Equal, But Italians Are Better

"Life is like a dogsled team. If you ain't the lead dog, the scenery never changes."

- Lewis Grizzard

My family always talked about race, religion, and ethnic backgrounds. There were ground rules in life but my grandparents taught my parents who taught us that ground rules were guidelines not straight jackets. They also taught us it's better if you're the one making the rules.

Don't judge someone by their religion, skin color, or where their grandparents came from. If they're good people that's all that counts. Just as members of my family were called "wops," (the slang term for "without papers" used for Italians emigrating to the U.S.), my family referred to others with similar unflattering terms. However, then it was more a way of life, used more to describe than to hurt or insult. Over the years when it became apparent that many people took offense to even unintended slurs, my parents respected the wishes of others and changed their vocabulary.

Open-mindedness seems to be a hallmark of outsiders. Immigrants and their families were outsiders so they learned to be like others to be accepted and to accept differences. Dressing differently is okay, going to worship on different days is okay, and even different wedding and funeral ceremonies were acceptable. The unspoken law was to be open-minded, don't criticize being different because different was the order of the day.

Likewise, by their very nature, immigrants and their families were risk takers. If you were brave enough to leave the old country with little more than a suitcase, what could be scary about working, opening a new business or anything else? Getting to America was the hard part. Everything else was a benefit for coming here.

In short, immigrants had common sense. They took risks. They experimented but were cautious. They looked back with fond memories but forward with great anticipation.

Perhaps one of the big mistakes we've made in America is to have allowed the melting pot to blend everyone into a homogeneous nation of people. The greatness of America is its diversity. Immigrants see things differently only because of their cultural differences. Immigrants have common sense. However, common sense is not always inherited.

Immigrants like immigrants. They enjoy sharing in each other's ceremonies of birth, death, marriage and religion. Italians especially liked celebrating the holidays of other nationalities. It was another excuse to eat.

Mom: "Today's St. Patrick's Day...I'll make a roast lamb...the Irish like lamb."

We didn't expect any Irishmen to come to dinner; we just ate on their behalf.

Mom: "Marvin is having his bar mitzvah...I'll make pork chops."

Vincent: "Mom, Jews don't eat pork."

Mom: "Are you going to Marvin's?"

Vincent: "No."

Mom: "Is Marvin coming here?"

Vincent: "No."

Mom: "So why can't we have pork chops?"

Or, for instance, on an Asian holiday we might get this logic.

Mom: "Today is Chinese New Year."

Vincent: "What's for dinner?"

Mom: "Fortune Roast."

Vincent: "Mom, the Chinese don't have fortune roast, they have fortune cookies."

Mom: "Listen, Mr. Big Shot, know it all about everything. The Chinese are fortunate to have anything. We're having fortune roast because it cost a fortune!"

To my parents, everyone was entitled to be what they were...Jews, Germans, Irish, Peruvian. It was okay to be another nationality. However, no matter what you were, my father believed there were really only two kinds of people in the world. Italians and those who wished they were Italian.

A few decades later, I moved to Oklahoma to attend college. Oklahoma is a wonderful part of Middle America, rich with the heritage of many tribes of Indians. Sadly, few of them are native to the area. Most were sent here against their will by the government.

Just as many long-established generations of Americans didn't appreciate the immigrants, (imagine if the Indians had treated the pilgrims that way), the government and white settlers of Oklahoma weren't very generous to the Indians. Since I come from an ethnic background, I pay particular attention to lifestyles and cultures of people. I noted early on, that nearly everyone in Oklahoma claimed to be part Indian. In the movies, Indians were "red" skinned with dark hair. Yet, in Oklahoma, six foot six, blue-eyed blondes named Chip claimed to be part Indian. It didn't take me long to figure out why.

The government pays people claiming to be even a fraction Indian a kind of restitution for abusing and destroying their culture. I'm not sure the government describes it that way, but that's what it appears to be as far as I'm concerned. Once I figured out I could get paid for being Indian I jokingly began to tell people I was half Italian and half Arapaho Indian...thus making me a "WOPAHOE." A few Indian friends and I have mused that with better connections to Italians, the Indians would have controlled all of the oil business (okay - so maybe it would have been the 'olive oil' business!) and casinos west of the Mississippi. Had they become Catholic, they would own the bingo business as well!

The Indian cultures are on the mend. Many tribes are working to restore their lifestyles, traditions, languages, alphabets, clothing and worship. The rest of us could learn a lot from the Indians, especially when it comes to dealing with nature. It was the Indians; after all, that helped those early immigrants coming to America make it through the winter.

Somehow that was forgotten in later years when they were run out of New England. Ironically, the Indians have created one of, if not the most profitable casinos in America in Connecticut. Turn around is fair play. Chalk one up for the Indians.

> "Love your enemies just in case your friends turn out to be a bunch of bastards."
> - R. A. Dickson

9 Judge And Jury

"Few things are more satisfying than seeing your children have teenagers of their own."

- Doug Larson

My folks believed in equal justice under "their" law. Whenever I got in trouble, they convened court.

Pop: "State your case, that's enough...you're guilty."

One time when I was a kid, my friend and I climbed on top of a beach house and peeled shingles off the roof to scale into the water. It was great fun until the police arrived and took us not to the police station but worse, home. About this time I started praying, "Hello God, my name's Vincent and I'm in a little trouble. If you get me out of this I'll become a priest."

As we walked toward the front door, Mom came outside clearly upset.

Mom: "Vincent, what happened? You okay?"

Vincent: "I'm fine, Mom."

Police: "Are you Mrs. Orza?" said the cop.

Mom: "Am I Mrs. Orza? Are you Sherlock Holmes? What happened to my son?"

Mom never answered a question with a statement. Immigrant logic: Always answer a question with a question and admit nothing.

Police: "Mrs. Orza, I arrested your son for destroying private property."

Mom: "What property?"

Police: "He and another kid were on the roof of a beach house tearing off shingles and scaling them into the water."

Mom: "My son knows better, it must have been the other kid. Why don't you go arrest him and leave my son alone?"

Mom could have played in the NFL as a quarterback for the Giants. This lateral pass of guilt (delegating blame) to the neighbor's kid must have worked because I don't remember being imprisoned or executed for this alleged crime.

Only later did I realize my Mother's objective was to get the cop to leave me home without a police escort. Mom knew she couldn't kill me with a witness...especially the police. As soon as the cop left, she began to circle her prey.

Mom: "What are you, crazy? Do you want to make me gray? Keep it up young man and you'll miss me when I'm gone. Did you have fun getting arrested?"

Vincent: "No."

Then came the real threat.

Mom: "Wait 'till your father gets home."

Wait 'till your father gets home meant she would torture me, he would do the killing.

I was banished to my room (which in those days had no radio, TV, stereo, books, games or anything else). It was a monk's cell - twin beds and a ceiling to stare at while I waited for Conan the Barbarian Father to come home and kill me. When Pop arrived, Mom "The Defender" from the police; became Mom, "The Prosecutor."

Mom: "Your son got in trouble today."

When I was in trouble, I was only my father's son. Mom didn't have any blood relation to bad kids.

Pop: "What kind of trouble?"

Mom: "Police trouble."

Storm clouds formed quickly when the word police was used in our house. Pop instantly called me to convene his "Kangaroo Court."

Pop: "Vincent - come out here, Bub."

My room bordered the dining room where my parents' discussion was being held. (Actually given the size of our house my room bordered every other room in the house!) I decided the best defense was a good offense. Being confined to my cell (bedroom) with nothing to do meant I obviously could have fallen into a deep sleep and thus would have been unable to hear Pop calling me. So I began to snore like a 75-year-old man. Despite my best acting, Pop wasn't buying.

Pop: "Get the hell out here before I come in there and bring you out."

I understand persuasive discussion so I woke up and went to the dining room to greet the man I worshiped.

Vincent: "Hi, daddy."

It didn't work, he was still mad.

Pop: "Your mother says (now I was her kid) you got in trouble with the police today."

Vincent" "Yes, sir."

Pop: "What are you, crazy?"

Are you crazy was a common question to me as a kid. It often came coupled with "What the hell's wrong with you?" or "Are you trying to make me spank you? Do you want to embarrass the Orza name, because if you want me to spank you I will?"

Lest you get confused, Pop also believed the Orza name to be very important. I had not thought of Orza's as comparable to Kennedy's or Rockefellers. Unfortunately, Pop did. It was his name and I had shamed it.

Vincent: "No, sir."

Pop: "No, sir what?"

Vincent: "No, sir. I don't want a spanking."

Pop: "Do you want a shot in the ass?

Shot in the ass meant spanking...it could also be a "shot in the head" or just "shot." In all cases, it meant trouble and asking me if I'd like one was his approach to democracy. I could pick my poison.

I only got spanked twice in my life. The threat of a spanking and the ritual that proceeded the spanking was usually enough to make me straighten up and fly right.

Pop, fingering the one-inch leather belt around his waist:

Pop: "Do you want a shot in the ass?"

Vincent: "No, sir."

Pop: "If you want one I'll give you one. Do you want one?"

I hadn't changed my mind.

Vincent: "No, sir."

Pop: "So why else would you embarrass your mother and me (I had two parents again) by making the police come to our house. You must want a spanking."

His hands were on the buckle.

Vincent: "No, sir."

Pop: "When I was a kid, I never made the police come to see my father. Do you know what Grandpa would have done to me if the police brought me home?"

I did. This was another story I'd heard and been threatened with on a few other occasions, but I lied.

Vincent: "No, sir."

Then I waited to hear the Grandpa shaving strap story again.

Pop: "Grandpa had a strap hanging that he used to sharpen his razor on. God help me if Grandpa had to use it on me."

This story lasted anywhere from a minute to 15 minutes, depending on the severity of my crime. Police at home was severe. The story, by the way, had two purposes. First, to make me feel guilty for embarrassing the family name and second, to give me time to make my final confession to God so I could enter Heaven without delay after Pop killed me.

Well, I lived through my first spanking and I learned to think twice before having fun. I still make mistakes, but I remember Pop and Grandpa's strap when I'm doing it.

"Remember that a kick in the ass is a step forward."
- John Chaucer

10 Blood Is Thicker Than Water...But

"I was going to buy a copy of the Power of Positive Thinking, and then I thought; what the hell good would that do?"

- Ronnie Shakes

My folks had ground rules for everything: no dinner...no dessert, bad grades...no TV, dirty room...clean the garage, get in trouble at school...grounded until the age of 30. We also had one other rule:

Rule #7: **Kid's don't argue or wise-off with adults! (Remember the name of the book!)**

One day when I was in my late seven's, I was a wise guy at school. My teacher made me stand in the corner where I continued to be a smart alec. He finally put me out in the hall and kind of gave me a real light slap in the back of the head (not equal to a "shot in the head," that was reserved for Pop). Now, a smart kid would have left it at that. Not me.

I remember my father saying he was the only one authorized to hit me. He had only once...until that day.

I came home from school and waited for Pop. When we were all sitting at the dinner table, I decided it was time to get my teacher in trouble with Pop.

By the way, we never ate before Pop got home.

Vincent: "Mom, what time is dinner?"

Mom: "When your father gets home."

I never found that spot on the clock!

Anyway, I decided to let my father know that my teacher had hit me, knowing my father would come to my aid and beat the hell out of this potential child-beating teacher. After all, blood is thicker than water.

Pop:	"What do you mean, your teacher hit you?"
Vincent:	"He hit me."
Pop:	"For what?"
Vincent:	"For nothing."

At that moment, I felt my bubble burst. It had not occurred to me I'd have to tell both sides of the story... much less the truth!

Like lightning, Pop reached across the table and gave me a shot across the back of my head. For those of you keeping score, I had now been hit twice (once by my teacher and once by Pop) for the same crime. Double jeopardy!

Pop:	"What do you mean for nothing. Mr. What's His Name wouldn't hit you for no reason."

It occurred to me to try logic.

Vincent:	"I didn't do anything. Who you gonna believe, him or me?"

Wrong question. Blood may be thicker than water, but it only matters if you are right. After I had a chance to explain the whole story, my father, a.k.a. the judge and jury ruled.

Pop:	"So you were being a wise guy, huh?"

And then I got a lecture and a spanking. Double jeopardy was now triple jeopardy. By the way, I also got sent to bed without supper. A suitable sentence for a wise guy.

The next morning the horror of uncontrolled justice continued.

Pop:	"Come on, I'll take you to school."

Now this was a real danger signal. My father never took me to school.

Vincent:	"No, Pop, that's okay. I'll walk."
Pop:	"Get in the car."

I didn't argue. At school we went to visit you-know-who. My father asked him about the previous day's incident. Needless to say, he remembered the event in much greater detail than I had. What's worse, he told the truth.

Teacher:	"Your son was being a wise guy."

Pop was steaming but he did eventually come to my defense.

Pop:	"If my kid's a problem you tell me. Don't ever lay a hand on him."

Way to go, Pop. Protect your son.

> Pop: "You tell me if he's out of line and I'll make sure it never happens again."

Then my father turned his attention to me.

> Pop: "And as for you, Bub, I don't have time to be coming down here to find out you can't behave yourself."

It occurred to me to explain that I hadn't asked him to come down there but I decided to leave well enough alone. Unfortunately for me, the incident wasn't over. I received another spanking when Pop got home that night. Is that quadruple jeopardy? The moral to this story wasn't to stay out of trouble; it was to never again tell my father I got in trouble at school. Second-generation logic!

As a kid I knew my parents would always defend me. My father and mother believed you stand by your family.

If someone accused me of something, Mom came to my defense. I often thought that had I been an axe murderer, Mom would have said, "But he's very neat. He doesn't get blood on the carpet or make a mess." While she might defend me in front of a stranger, there would be hell to pay when we got home.

Actually, the real hell was my parents telling me that I disappointed them or worse yet, that they were ashamed of me. I would rather have gotten a spanking, but Pop and Mom had a rule for that.

Rule #8: Shame is worse than pain.

I also learned that while blood may be thicker than water, adults stick together, especially when it comes to wise-ass kids.

"Conscience is the inner
voice that warns us
somebody may be looking."
                - H.L. Mencken

11 Stop That Damn Swearing

"Ye shall know the truth, and the truth shall make you mad."

- Aldous Huxley

I come from a family that swears. We don't do it to offend anyone. We're just colorful speakers. When I moved to Oklahoma, I realized that not everyone considered swearing so acceptable. The strong Baptist influence did help to cleanse mid-western language but not necessarily their thoughts. I learned Yankees were more direct. Middle America may swear less, but committed just as many other sins. Hell and damn are second nature to my vocabulary but less common in Oklahoma. Just as my family adjusted its vocabulary relative to immigrants, I've tried to modify mine for geography.

When I was about ten, I learned another word that was taboo if used incorrectly. The word is Mother. The only time I ever really saw my father mad, real mad, enraged, was one day at work when he was in the middle of a conversation with a customer. The other guy said something that really infuriated my father. Pop struck like lightening and decked the guy with one punch. Everyone in sight stopped to see what had happened as Pop turned and walked away form the guy lying on the floor, seeing stars.

Years later, my father told me why he hit the guy. My father wasn't offended by most swear words. However, my father, like a lot of men, loved his mother like a saint. Men swearing at each other was one thing - men using the word Mother with a particular swear word was quite another. Take it from me, don't ever use the word mother incorrectly around my dad or you'll wind up lying on the floor. Pop had his principles and if someone crossed the line, they'd know it.

Swearing in the fifties was pretty tame. It seems we were less puritanical then. Hell and damn were acceptable language but Ricky and Lucy Ricardo couldn't be seen sleeping in the same bed on TV. Movie directors had the good sense to fade to black as scenes rather than people climaxed.

People called each other a son-of-a-bitch or a bastard during an argument but real vulgarity was unheard of. Language today is pretty vulgar and it's used by nearly everyone.

I can remember testing the language waters as I grew up. I didn't have to swear to catch hell from my mother. When I did say something she didn't like (such as the word "NO"), the punishment was swift and clean. She washed my mouth out with soap. It only happened once or twice and I learned to think first and speak second.

Years later, my wife decided to invoke the same punishment on one of our daughters for saying something Patti considered unacceptable. I believe it was "no" when Patti wanted "yes." She dragged our first born into the bathroom and proceeded to give her teeth and tongue a nice fresh soaping. Unbeknownst to Patti, our youngest daughter Alix was standing there watching the whole procedure.

A few days later, Alix walked into the kitchen with a mouth full of soap. Patti asked her what happened. Alix explained that she had said something she shouldn't have...and washed her own mouth out with soap as punishment. In immigrant logic, this is explained as "the apple doesn't fall too far from the tree."

As a kid, I was often confused as to who I was. Apparently, Bill Cosby had the same problem. Based on what Cosby said, we may have the same father. Bill says as a kid, he thought his name was "Jesus Christ" and his brother was "Damn it" because that's what his father called him. My dad did the same thing.

Pop would often shout, "Jesus Christ, get over here."

"Jesus Christ, are you crazy?"

"Jesus Christ, what's wrong with you?"

When I wasn't Jesus Christ, I was Damn it.

"Damn it, don't do that."

"Damn it, were you raised in a barn?"

As an adult, swearing still was not a big thing to me; at least it wasn't until I had my kids. You learn not to swear when your own kids embarrass you in church. It happened to me one Sunday morning when my beautiful, adorable, precious little daughter dropped one of her toys in church. Trust me, there's nothing worse than seeing everyone in the building turn towards you when your beautiful, adorable, precious little daughter says, "damn."

I'm certain she must have learned it from my wife!

Right then and there, I decided to try and stop that Damn Swearing! I'm still trying!

"Many of life's failures are people who did not realize how close they were to success when they gave up."
- Thomas Edison

12 Some - "Things"

"Should a thief threaten to blow out your brains if
you don't turn over your money, give him your
brains. You can live in this world without brains, but
not without money."

- Sam Levenson

I remember a woman comedian on the Ed Sullivan show
telling about her family. It sounded like ours.

Wife to
Husband:	"What do you want to eat?"
Husband:	"Anything."
Wife:	"Like what?"
Husband:	"Anything."
Wife:	"How about a sandwich?"
Husband:	"Fine."

About that time their kid walks in and tells the mother, "I'm
hungry."

Wife:	"What do you want to eat?"
Kid:	"I don't know, something."
Wife:	"Oh no, I'm not cooking two dinners...you'll have what your father's eating."

Long ago, I decided people reach a certain age and they go to
parent's school. It's where we all learn to say things parents say.
My mother has her favorites such as "I don't care what everyone
else is doing, everyone else is not my kid. If everyone else jumps
off a bridge, are you going to jump off a bridge too?" Or if I was
flirting with trouble, I got something like this from Pop. "Hey -
do you want a spanking? If you want a spanking, I'll give you one.
Tell me, do you want a spanking? You're making me mad just

talking about a spanking. Come over here so I can break both of your legs!" The worst part is, I went!

Let me ask you something, did your mom tell you your room looked like a pigsty? My mom came from New York City. How did she even know what a pigsty looked like? How about this, did your father ever say, "Don't make me come over there?" Jay Leno always jokes about his dad saying what my dad said, "I'll turn this car around right now and we'll just stay home." I'm convinced these are all things learned at parent's school somewhere in Montana.

When I did the normal dumb stuff kids do or said something I shouldn't have; I got this:

Pop or Mom:	"Hey, you got something to say young man?"
Vince:	"No."
Pop or Mom:	"Then say it."
Vince:	"Huh?"
Pop or Mom:	"Don't you look at me in that tone of voice, you speak when you're spoken to!"
Vince:	"But."
Pop or Mom:	"That's it, I've heard enough. Go to your room."

Grooming was also a constant topic.

Pop:	"Hey Bub. You need a haircut."
Vince:	"My hair is not long!"
Pop:	"According to who?"
Vince:	"According to no-body. My hair is fine."
Pop:	"Well I'm somebody and you're no-body and this is no democracy. I'm telling nobody to mind his or her own business. Get your ass to the barbershop."

I'm sure you're all familiar with this old favorite:

Vince:	"Mom can I go to the beach?"
Mom:	"Not now."
Vince:	"Oh Mom- why not?"
Mom:	"Because I said so!"
Vince:	"But Mom."

Mom:	"Don't 'But Mom me' I said no."
Vince:	"But Mom - why not?"
Mom:	"I told you because I said so and I'm the Mom. When you grow up you'll be the Mom and then you can say so...until then I'm the Mom!"

My mother had some great one-liners. Things she said that always made you stop and think. There was the time my sister Connie and mother were arguing. My mother took off a shoe and threw it at my sister. Connie ducked and the shoe hit the wall knocking down a plate from my mother's collection. The plate hit the floor and shattered...Mom's response was simple. "Look what you made me do." This is referred to as DELEGATING BLAME!

The best line my mother learned at Mom's school in Montana is "You'll miss me when I'm gone." It was invoked when I needed something. "Mom's where's my clean underwear?" "You'll miss me when I'm gone." "Mom, what's for dinner?" "You'll miss me when I'm gone." My mother's been using this line for 70+ years and you know she's right.

In hindsight, I helped make my mother a little crazy. I was forever playing tricks on her. Once while Mom was preparing macaroni for dinner, she took the pot and poured its contents into a colander to drain. As she turned around to put the hot empty pot back on the stove, I grabbed the pasta and quickly hid it in the oven.

As Mom turned back around to finish preparing the macaroni, she stopped cold looking for the colander she had just put in the sink to drain. She quickly looked back at the pot. Then for some reason she looked in two or three of the cabinets, the refrigerator and on the dining room table all the while never saying a word.

Pop and I were trying our best not to laugh or ask any questions that would let on we had conspired to drive her crazy. While she searched, I grabbed the macaroni from the oven and put it back in the sink. When she turned back around, there was the pasta. She never looked up, questioned where it had been or acknowledged it was missing. She did mumble to herself about being absent minded and going crazy.

A few years ago, we were all sitting at the table having dinner. I was reminiscing about my grandmother. I was telling my girls that my grandmother always wore her hair up in a bun. Only once in my life had I seen Grandma with her hair down and I was surprised that it reached all the way down her back. Mom then explained "Grandma only had long hair until she cut it." I'll never forget the look on our faces as we tried to make sense of Mom's logic.

"I'm silent because I discipline myself to only speak when it will be an improvement on silence."
- Calvin Coolidge

13 Sex...Thank God For Barbershops

"On Sex Education: Let them teach it! If the schools teach sex the way they teach everything else, the kid's lose interest anyhow."

- Sam Levenson

It always amazed me how so many kids hated to go to the barbershop. Not me. I thought the barbershop was the best adventure a kid could have. As a little kid, you went with your dad. At ten or twelve, you went all by yourself (no girls, no moms...just us men). Now, I'm about to disclose America's best-kept secret of the 1950's. Why did all us boys have short hair (burrs, flat tops, etc.) in the 50's? Think about it. Wally and Beaver Cleaver, Eddie Haskell, Rusty Williams (Danny Thomas' kid), and Jeff on *Donna Reed* all had short hair. The answer: *Playboy* magazine. All day long everyone at home, church and school said don't read *Playboy*. "Sex will make you go blind." "Looking at naked women is a sin." Yet, in the 1950's in barbershops across America there was *Playboy* magazine big as life, free and available for every kid to read.

Vince: "Mom, I think I need a haircut."

Mom: "Okay, here's a dollar. Go to the barber shop."

A week later.

Vince: "Mom, I need my flat top trimmed."

Mom: "Okay, here's a dollar. Go to the barber shop."

Let's face it fellows, the Beatles' long hair ruined years of great free *Playboy*. Women's lib didn't help either. Before women's lib, only men could cut men's hair. This was no accident. After all, in the 50's you couldn't read *Playboy* in front of a woman.

The other great bastion of male superiority was the work place. No one had sex at work, but everyone thought about it there. You see, during the first half of the century, men completely dominated the work force. When men went to work and left the women at home to do "women's work" the men could be tough.

It was easier to be tough in those days, because we didn't have the women around to call our bluff. The garage at the gas station, the parts counter at the hardware store and the bench at the shoemakers all had one thing in common. The calendar! Now I don't mean the bank or insurance company calendar. I mean the girly calendar you saw only at work. This piece of Americana went the way of the pen that had the woman in the bathing suit in it...the same pen that saw the bathing suit disappear when you turned it upside down.

The pen and the calendar both disappeared in the 1960's. That was about the same time a lot of boys lost interest in working and became hippies. Come to think of it, they gave up barbershops, the calendar and pen to be with girls who streaked and didn't wear bras. There is no particular immigrant logic to be applied here. My father just referred to them as "damn fools" but he did watch the news about hippies a little more closely, especially since there were no more girly calendars.

"You miss 100% of the shots you never take."
- Wayne Gretzky

14 Call Home

"Home is the place where, when you have to go there, they have to take you in."

- Robert Frost

One of the benefits of being the baby in the family is you learn what older brothers and sisters do that aggravate your parents. Kids, listen up. Mothers and fathers expect and appreciate a call. While they never told my brother or sister they didn't call enough, they always told each other and me.

Mom: "Who was that?"

Pop: "Danny."

Mom: "What did he want?"

Pop: "Nothing, he just called to say hello."

Mom: "He must feel guilty for not calling more often. I could've died and he wouldn't even know."

Pop: "He called two days ago."

Mom: "That was then. What, I couldn't have died yesterday? He should call more often."

More often meant daily. More often than that if possible. I learned to call more often. Don't get me wrong, my parents don't mind calling us, they just expect us to call them more than they call us.

Rule #9: Age has rank.

Calling your parents is strange. Sometimes you call for no reason and they don't believe it.

Vincent: "Hi, Mom."

Mom: "Hi, who's this?"

I never understood this question. My folks have three kids (two boys and one girl) and obviously, I was not my sister, so they had a fifty-fifty chance, but they never risked it.

Vincent: "It's Vincent."

Mom: "What's up with you?"

Vincent: "Nothing, I just called to say hi."

Mom: "Where are you?"

Notice all of the questions implied I might want something ...what's up...or put another way, whatsa matter. Where are you really means - did you get arrested?

Mom: "Anything wrong?"

Vincent: "No I'm fine."

Mom: "Have you eaten?" This was their way of inviting me over.

Vincent: "No, not yet."

Mom: "Why don't you come over? I've got a roast, some macaroni, soup and salad in the refrigerator."

My mother always had more food in the refrigerator than the Queen Mary had in its kitchen.

Vincent: "No, I'll stop and get something at the store."

Mom: "The store! The store's got junk. Eat here. I'll warm something up."

I generally gave in because by the time we finished discussing eating, it was time for another meal.

Mom: "So, why did you call?"

Vincent: "I just called to say hello."

Mom: "You didn't just call to say hello yesterday."

Vincent: "I was busy yesterday."

Mom: "My son the big shot...too busy to call his mother and say hello. What were you too busy doing yesterday that you couldn't call?"

Vincent: "I was working."

Mom:	"What, you dig ditches, are you a sailor...you're a teacher doctor, you're in an office? Ditch diggers and sailors don't call because they don't have phones in the ditch or in the ocean. What, there's no phones in your office?"
Vincent:	"I'm sorry, Mom, I'll call more often."
Mom:	"More often may be too late next time. You'll miss me when I'm gone...then you'll wish you had called more often."

By the way, in case you are wondering about me being a teacher doctor, I have an Ed.D. There are medical doctors (MD's), Doctors of Philosophy (Ph.D.'s) and Doctor of Education (Ed.D.'s). An Ed.D. is the same as a Ph.D. without any foreign languages as a part of their course work.

Mom never quite got the Ed.D. She knew doctors were physicians. Some even specialized their practice; to her I was a specialist. I had my doctorate in Education. I was..."A doctor for teachers!"

"Have you ever been treated by a doctor?" "No. I always paid for it."
- Will Rogers

15 You Can't Do That

"Never give in. Never. Never. Never. Never."
                                — Winston Churchill

My parents never told me I couldn't do something. They might question why I wanted to do something, the benefit, the purpose, the logic, (theirs, not mine), but never said no, don't.

They negotiated terms and conditions, laid down ground rules and then lit a candle and prayed their kid was smart enough to not get arrested or killed.

Vincent: "Pop, can I go to Europe?"

Pop: "You gotta go to school."

Vincent: "After school."

Pop: "You've got homework."

Vincent: "No, during the summer with my teacher, Mr. Bosshardt. He's taking a bunch of kids to study in Europe."

Pop: "What is he rich?"

Vincent: "We pay our own way. It's a thousand dollars for two months."

Pop: "That's a good deal. You got a thousand dollars?"

Vincent: "No."

Pop: "So how you gonna get to Europe."

Vincent: "I'll get it."

Pop: "How, rob a bank?"

Vincent: "I'll work. You've taught me to save."

I had learned over the years the trick of making the other guy feel important by telling him you'd learned from him. Pop, I'm sure, knew I had a couple of hundred bucks in the bank and was headed to college. His next response was relatively safe.

Pop:	"You think you can save that much money by summer?"
Vincent:	"Yes...but I may need a loan."

Pop's no fool. "Banks don't loan kids vacation money."

Vincent:	"I was thinking of you."
Pop:	"Thanks for thinking of me...I'll think about you."

My father and mother are two brave souls. They talked it over and even told my grandmother. All agreed the trip would be a wonderful education. My grandmother spoke no English other than yes, no, thank you and doggie. Doggie meant Lassie on TV. Every Sunday night at seven o'clock, she pointed to the TV and said "Doggie." Grandma told me in Italian how excited she was that I would be the first in two generations to go see her homeland.

She also slipped me a one hundred-dollar bill for spending money. My grandmother hadn't left our house without us for years. To this day, I don't know where she got the money, much less a hundred-dollar bill. Years later when my folks sold the house and moved out, it really bothered me that somewhere in that house, there was a brick with God knows how much money behind it.

The trip to Europe was to follow my high school graduation, which was no certain thing. I was a lousy student up through my junior year in high school. Basically, I didn't pay attention. The Vietnam War was raging and everyone knew if it wasn't college, it was Southeast Asia. When my guidance counselor told me, "Vincent, you are not college material," she more or less told me I shouldn't even try to get in. What's worse, she said if I were lucky enough to get in I'd never finish. I was mad and insulted.

My folks, all of my family and I were typical immigrants. We believed we could do anything if we set our mind to it. That's why we came to America. The words of my guidance counselor were all the challenge I needed. Life has a strange way of turning out for the best. In my senior year of high school, I took my first big risk in life...I ran for president of my senior class.

The kids in my high school were supposed to ride the bus to school, yet everyday most of us drove our cars and parked them in the grocery store lot across the street. I guess we assumed the school administration and grocery storeowner wouldn't notice our 200 cars appear each day at 7:30 in the morning.

I was relatively new to the school and couldn't figure out why with that big parking lot on campus; we all parked in the grocery store lot. One day I asked our principal why all the kids had to park off campus. His response taught me a lesson… "No one asked permission to park on campus." So I asked, "If I run for President of my class and win, can we park on campus?" "Sure," he replied.

So, that day I announced my candidacy for president of the senior class. The kid who was president of the junior class expected to be elected president of the senior class. I ran on the platform, "Vote for me and I'll get you parking privileges." It worked! I won; I was elected class president.

Orza's law…you don't know what's possible until you try. My guidance counselor still didn't think college was a good idea for me. She was convinced I'd fail.

By the grace of God, a few great teachers, threat of war, and by virtue of the fact I was now President of my class and didn't want to look like a fool, my grades improved. God has a strange way of watching over us. Being President of my senior class wound up getting me a few shots at college. Oklahoma City University (a small Methodist college trying to fill its Catholic Italian quota) recruited me because as President of my senior class, I was a "leader." I would go there immediately upon my return from Europe.

As a result of my trip to Europe, I grew up. I quickly realized how beautiful the world was and how fortunate I was to be an American. I also developed an appreciation for history, art and gardens. I stayed in Europe longer than I expected and didn't get to Oklahoma City until January 1969. I transferred in about twelve hours of college credit and completed four years of college in two and one-half years. So much for my guidance counselor's assessment of my ability!

My folks always told me what I'm sure their folks told them, "You can do better." No matter how good something is, it can still be better. My grades were lousy until my junior year in high school.

Pop: "You can do better, Vincent."

Vincent: "Okay, Pop."

My grades got better.

Pop: "You can still do better, Vincent."

Vincent: "Okay, Pop."

Finally, one semester in my senior year, I got straight A's. I knew my father would be proud. That's when I learned about justifiable homicide. My sister was always the whiz kid. My father definitely loved his daughter.

"Pop, I got straight A's." My father looked at me, at my report card, and said, "You know, your sister always got straight A's." Grounds for justifiable homicide! It's not that Pop wasn't proud of me. He said, "I knew you could do better, you just figured it out."

Rule #10:   **If anyone tells you don't try, tell them to drop dead. Pop was right. You can do better, but only if you try.**

"The guy on top of the mountain didn't fall there."
- Vince Orza

16 Hot Line To God

"Lead your life so you wouldn't be ashamed to sell the family parrot to the town gossip."

- Will Rogers

My family took their kids to everything, including funerals. For Italians, funerals are not only good-byes to yesterday but hello to tomorrow. "Hey, life goes on."

I never knew my father's parents. They passed away before I was born. Both my mother's parents lived longer lives than my Pop's and they lived the last five to ten years of their lives with us. When your grandparents live with you, death is harder to overcome but expected. I was close to Grandma and Grandpa. They spoke very little English but even as a little kid, we all understood each other. I always sat on their laps. They bounced me on their knees and we laughed. Grandma seemed to always have rosary beads in her hands as she silently prayed for everyone and everything. Grandma spoke to God like they were best friends.

When Grandma and Grandpa lived in New York, they would sit on a small bench outside in front of their railroad flat apartment opposite the church. A railroad flat is a long narrow apartment. To get to the living room, you had to walk through the bedroom. There was a crucifix in every room. Every time Grandma would go from one room to another, she'd kiss her hand and touch it to the crucifix (Immigrant logic: God needs love too). Grandpa made wine in the basement. Their bathroom had a toilet and tub - no shower or sink. My grandfather had a small garden in the back. He harvested enough fruit and vegetables to feed a small Central American nation. All my memories of Grandma are in the kitchen. Day or night, we all wound up at the kitchen table to eat and talk.

As immigrants go, my grandparents were the same as millions of others that came to the New World for a chance. They expected nothing but an opportunity and refused handouts because their pride was bigger than their stomach. Immigrants are ingenious people. One chicken could feed a family of ten and the bones made soup for the next night.

They worked day and night; seven days a week, never missed mass or a chance to light a candle or a quick prayer. The faith and success of immigrants in this nation would make you believe they had a hot line to God. I know my grandparents did.

Grandpa died a slow, agonizing death of cancer. He was tough till the end. He never understood why he couldn't die at home. Hospitals were for sick people, home was where you lived and died.

My father really liked his father-in-law. At Grandpa's funeral, Pop paid a silent tribute to the tough old man who was always warm and friendly. I remember my father walking up to Grandpa as he lay in the casket and reaching over to touch the old man. "Good-bye, Pop" were my father's only words.

From that moment on, my father knew his responsibility was to care for Grandma and he did. Many years later after my grandmother had lived with us for a long time, my mother had no choice but to confine her to a nursing home. It was more painful for my mother than grandmother. Mom felt she was letting her mother down when in reality; my grandmother (all 200 pounds of her) needed constant care. Pop and Mom spent their life savings keeping my grandmother comfortable in that nursing home.

I watched my mother grow old trying to do the impossible for my grandmother. Years later, Grandma died. I loved her the way everyone should love their Grandma. Immigrants expect to take care of their own. It's a lesson many of us could learn.

By the way, Grandma's hot line to God is alive and well. Whenever I go to mass, I say a prayer for my grandparents.

> "Hi, Grandma, it's me, Vincent. How's things in Heaven? Mom's fine. I miss you. Hey, God, please keep an eye on Grandma and Grandpa and my folks and Patti and Patti's Mom and please, please, please always watch over Landi and Alix (our two daughters). Thanks God, bye Grandma."

I'm convinced God is pretty smart. He understands all languages, can hear silence, can see in the dark and is a great guy (or girl). He doesn't need fancy smancy churches, or stand on ceremony, but he does appreciate hearing from us. God and my parents have the same philosophy – "call often." Most important, He does answer prayers.

Case in point. Several years ago, my father was diagnosed with cancer. My father's never had more than a cold in his life. Neither did his father. When I was a kid, Pop told us stories about the man we called Grandpa Orza. He smoked short, stubby Italian cigars about the quality of a rope. They were called ginny stinkers. Grandpa Orza ate whatever he pleased, smoked like a chimney and drank wine with lunch and dinner everyday of his life. No cancer, no high cholesterol, no heart condition, no hemorrhoids, no ingrown toenails. Nothing. He died healthy as a horse of old age.

My father told us stories about Grandpa Orza's silky, soft hair. When my father went in the hospital for surgery with his cancer, I flew to Florida to be with him. He picked me up at the airport and we drove to the hospital together. It was one of the toughest moments of my life.

Pop: "Your Mom's gonna need your help, Bub."

Vincent: "I know, Pop. I'll take care of everything until you're back on your feet."

Pop handed me the key to his safe deposit box, his life insurance policy, and his checkbook.

Pop: "Your mother's never written a check, doesn't know anything about paying bills, the life insurance or any of that."

Pop was preparing me for his potential visit to see his parents and my mother's parents in God's backyard. I wasn't ready for him to make the trip. After surgery, I sat holding my father in my arms as he slept in the recovery room. I stroked his hair. It was silky soft just like Grandpa Orza's. As I held him in my arms, I placed a long distanced conversation to God.

"Hello, God, this is Vincent. I'm the kid that ripped the shingles off the roof of the beach house a few years ago. Remember me, I promised to be a priest if you helped me out of that jam. God, I need your help again today. This one's more serious. God, this is my father. He thinks you're ready to cash in his chips. God, not now. I know you're God and you know what you're doing, but I need my father a little longer. I want my daughters to have a Grandpa for a while. If you give him a job in Heaven, my kids won't ever know what it's like to sit on Grandpa's knee and be bounced. Grandpa's supposed to be there for Santa Claus, to cut the Thanksgiving turkey, for their first communion, to play with in the pool.

God, I know you don't make mistakes, but could it be the guy you want right now is someone else. Someone with older grandchildren who has done all this stuff already? How about double-checking the records because I really need Pop a little longer? Don't take my dad...not now."

The hot line worked. Pop's alive and well. Every night when I kiss my girls good night, I also thank God. I'll bet Pop does too.

Rule #11:   Depend on God.

"We should work as if we will live 100 years but pray as though we may die tomorrow."

- Ben Franklin

17 Marriage...Battle Of The Sexes

"The hardest thing to do in life is to learn which bridge to cross and which to burn."

- David Russell

As a kid, I always enjoyed stories about my folks, jokes about marriage and the kibitzing between husband and wife. Trust me; those stories and experiences are more enjoyable to kids because they are not married.

I've been married twice. I married young to a first rate girl I'd gone to high school with. You can't tell kids about marriage. They don't believe you, they think they're smarter than everyone else is and they believe love will conquer all. Sometimes it doesn't.

I'm sure age and maturity impacts the selection of one's wife or husband. I was crushed from my divorce, convinced I should stay single, yet lonely for the friendship, love and companionship I had lost. My decision to remarry was correct. Bells went off, stars came out, fireworks lighted the sky, and I fell in love.

There's no question about it; love is lovelier the second time around. I'm a hopeless romantic. I met Patti at a pretty lousy time in my life. Actually, I met her years before when she was a student of mine at the University. I was married at the time and she was engaged. I actually hired her to do some modeling for a few of my advertising clients. She took two classes with me (she got one A and one B and I've caught hell over that B ever since. If I had known I was going to fall in love and marry her, I would have given her two A's.) After she finished school I didn't see her again for two years.

One day while shopping, I bumped into her. Unfortunately, I didn't recognize her and she had to remind me that I had been her professor. She had cut her hair and looked different. Terrific, but different. By the way, I've caught hell about not remembering her but I've tried to explain to Patti I only remembered straight "A" students. Sad to say, this argument hasn't helped me either. When your wife's been your student and you give her a B and then forget who she is...you're a marked man for life.

Two weeks after we had met again, I worked up enough nerve to call her for a date. Well, actually I worked up enough nerve and an excuse to call her.

Vincent: "Hi...this is Vince Orza. Do you still do any
            modeling work?"

Yes, I know this is one of the lamest excuses for a date, but I was convinced she'd tell me to drop dead. Thankfully, she didn't laugh in my face or I would have hung up and gone to a monastery for a quiet life of embarrassment.

Patti: "Oh, not really. Why, do you need a model?

Vincent: "Yes, how about meeting me for dinner?"

I know - why do models have to have dinner with agency people. Hey, I was a jerk trying to convince a beautiful girl to go out with me.

Well, thank God she went out with me. Like everyone who falls in love at first sight, I was a klutz. However, I did try to turn on the charm. When I picked her up, I brought one red rose. Very suave, (and also cheaper than a dozen). The day after our dinner, she left town on business. She went to New York and despite the fact that New York City has nine million people; I was able to track her down.

I sent a telegram to her hotel.

"Had a great time at dinner. Looking forward to seeing you again. Give me a call when you return and I'll pick you up at the airport."

I sent a telegram thinking it would be very romantic. Well, actually I sent it because I'm a lousy conversationalist. I assumed she'd receive the telegram and call me. I was wrong.

Three days went by and I died of embarrassment every minute of those three days. No call. In my mind, I could see her in New York laughing at this jerk in Oklahoma that sent a telegram.

As it happens, it took her three days to get the telegram. When she got it, she called and the rest is history. I picked her up; we went out for dinner every day for seven months and got married. I had convinced her to spend her life with me or that I was in the

Mafia and I could have her snuffed out. I prefer to believe it was the first reason, but just in case, I watch the Godfather every time it's on TV. It makes her wonder!

In as much as I'm Italian and I can find someone visiting New York on business, my wife still wonders if all Italians are in the Mafia. I tell her it's best not to ask too many questions. It's the only chance I have to win an occasional argument with her.

Grandma and Grandpa Orza's courtship was a little different. Grandpa came to America alone as a young man before the turn of the century. His family had relatives here already. Grandpa came to establish a new life but shortly after he arrived, his father called him back to Italy to meet the girl they had picked out to be his wife.

So Grandpa crossed the Atlantic back to Italy to meet his wife to be. When he arrived home, he did not like his family's choice, so he came back to America a second time.

He was called back home again to meet the second choice that he once again decided was not the girl of his dreams. Sailing back to the states for the third time he met my grandmother. She was also being sent by her family to have a new, better life in America. Grandpa wired his father in Italy about the girl he'd met on the ship. Both their families had relatives in the U.S. who blessed the arrangement. So, Grandpa and Grandma Orza could get to work building a family. They succeeded with 7 kids.

No matter how old you are, bringing your future husband or wife home to meet your parents is awkward. After I asked Patti to marry me, I called my folks in Florida to tell them I was coming to visit and would be bringing a friend.

Mom: "Oh good. What's his name?"

Vincent: "Patti."

Mom: "What is he, Irish?"

Vincent: "No Mom, Patti is a girl."

Mom: "Oh…you're coming with a girl."

You could have cut the silence with a knife.

Vincent: "Yes."

Mom: "Why?"

Vincent: "To visit."

Mom: "Oh."

We flew to Florida. When we arrived, Mom and Pop were waiting. Patti is gorgeous so I knew Pop would be no problem. My mother, on the other hand, would protect her baby, even if he were 30.

We drove to their home talking about Patti, where she came from and all the rest of the rap sheet information necessary for any police inquiry. As much as I tried to protect her, I was no match for my mother the grand inquisitor.

Everything was going great until we pulled into the driveway. As we got out of the car, Pop started helping me unload our luggage. Always the gentlemen (especially with great looking blondes escorted by his son) Pop grabbed Patti's bags. As he was entering the house he paused.

Pop: "I'll put Patti's bags in Grandma's room.

(Grandma's room was hers even though she had died about five years earlier.)

Vincent: "That's fine, Pop. I'll sleep in the spare room; Patti can have Grandma's room.

Pop: "It's okay, you two can sleep..."

Vincent: "Not a problem Pop. I'll sleep in the spare room and Patti will take Grandma's."

Pop: "'Cause if you two want..."

Vincent: "Pop, Patti will stay in Grandma's room and I'll be in the spare room."

It was Pop's way of saying we were old enough to do whatever we liked. At the same time it was our way of saying, "Hey, this is your house and while we are under your roof, we'll play by your rules."

Each night when my folks were ready to go to sleep, we'd hear it again.

Pop: "Well your mother and I are going to bed. You kids can do whatever. We can't hear anything from the other side of the house."

Each morning Pop got up at his normal 5:00 a.m. As a Florida retiree, he felt compelled to squeeze fresh orange juice from his own tree. So bright and early we'd both awake to the grinding noise of the juicer. Pop would open the door just enough to say:

"Hey Bub, you awake? I got fresh orange juice for you."

"Patti, how about a nice glass of fresh orange juice?"

Needless to say, you couldn't refuse. So, up we were at 5:00 a.m. every morning. I told Patti she should visit with my mom about our wedding, but hadn't told Mom about that minor detail. Fortunately, Patti had the keys to my mother's heart. Patti wanted to be a mom. Once she told my mother she wanted to have kids, Mom dropped her guard.

I learned something extra special on that visit. Patti's father died a young man when she was only seven years old. She missed the wonderful experiences many girls have with their daddies. She helped me realize how lucky I was to have both my parents as a kid and as an adult. Patti and her mother are as close as any two people could be. I learned to be more appreciative of that as well. For as much as I always enjoyed my family, Patti helped me cherish them even more. Her ability to make our family and home so special won her a place in the "nearly Italian" Mom and Pop Orza Hall of Fame.

To qualify, you have to want to have and then have kids. You have to learn to cook Italian food like my mother and you have to keep a house clean enough to make the cover of Good Housekeeping magazine. Patti was a gold medal winner in each category. Hence even though she's a French, German, Bohemian and God knows what else, (all of which are akin to Huns, Visigoths and barbarians to Italians), she has been given the official "Good Housekeeping Seal of Approval" by Mom and Pop…oh yeah, and me.

"It is often easier to fight for one's principles than to live up to them."

- Adlai Stevenson

18 It's Not Intelligent Vision

"The mind is like a TV set — when it goes blank, it's a good idea to turn off the sound."
                                        - Communication Briefings

When I was a kid, television was still a novelty. We had the first one on our block. In those days, the TV screen was very small so you had to put some sort of contraption fitted with oil in front of the screen to magnify the picture.

Of course I was the kid who knocked the thing over spilling the oil all over the living room floor. I was either too young to get a spanking, or I got one so bad that I've blanked out that memory. In any case, we didn't watch much TV in those days because there wasn't much to watch. All the programming in the country totaled a few hours a day on one, two, or three channels.

What I did watch often wound up getting me in trouble.

As a kid I loved the *Three Stooges*. I would imitate their laughs, the routines clicking their fingers making a fist, poking guys in the eye, hitting them under the chin, that forward and backward skip and all the other funny but dumb stuff they did.

The problem was Pop didn't like me acting like an idiot and the *Three Stooges* were on TV right about the time Pop would get home from work.

Pop: "I'm home."

Mom: "Hello, ready for dinner?"

Pop: "Yep - what's to eat?"

Now I never understood this question. My mother had a routine. In our house, you could tell the day of the week by the food on the table. Friday, no meat, we were Catholic so we had fish. Saturday was steak night, Sunday was macaroni, Monday was soup, and Tuesday we got leftovers from the weekend.

Wednesday we usually got the weird stuff - liver or pig knuckles, and Thursdays was chicken. Yet night after night Pop would ask what's for dinner.

In those days, we (the kids) were supposed to go greet Pop at the door. The only time Pop came to find me was when I was in trouble.

Vincent: "Hi, Pop."

Pop: "Hello, Bub. What are you doing?"

My father asked me the same question every night, and I was dumb enough to answer.

Vincent: "Watching the *Three Stooges*."

And every night I'd hear,

Pop: "Turn that crap off. I don't want you watching those damn fools, acting like idiots. How many times do I have to tell you I don't want you watching that...?"

This went on for 10-15 minutes. As I got older, I finally learned to turn the Three Stooges off the moment I heard "I'm home." God only knows what Pop would tell his kids about the really stupid, violent trash on TV today.

TV was pretty wholesome in the 1950's. *Leave it to Beaver, Make Room for Daddy* and *Amos and Andy* were wonderful programs to learn from. I often wondered why *Amos and Andy* hasn't been brought back. I don't believe anyone ever thought of the program as one for just blacks anymore than Beaver was about white kids. On the contrary, they were programs about people. Programs about friends, family, and life's troubles but always with a happy ending.

I also watched *Abbott and Costello*. Only as an adult did I realize these two geniuses of comedy were at the close of their careers by the time they got to TV. Their years in the movies made them giants without having to be vulgar to be hilarious.

It really was a more innocent time. We had Ed Sullivan (who introduced the nation to Elvis Presley...but covered the screen from the waist down so America couldn't see him swivel his hips.) We had Red Skelton with the seagulls Gertrude and Heathcliff, Clem Kadidelhopper and Freddie the Freeloader. The serious stuff included *Zane Grey Theater, Dragnet* and of course *Lassie*. Crimes were always solved, murders had no blood, bad guys were locked up and good guys got the happy endings.

My grandmother never quite understood television. After all, when she came to America there was no electricity, no radio, no TV, no running water, no airplanes and no cars. She grew up with horse and buggies, trains and boats. Television confounded her. She thought there really were tiny people inside that big box.

When America sent the first man to the moon and television showed Neil Armstrong hopping around up there, my mother and I tried to explain to Grandma what was happening. She thought we were teasing her. She told me she wasn't stupid and knew you couldn't get to the moon. We persisted and she decided to catch us in our own joke. She asked how long it took to get there. We said a few days. She asked where did they stop for gas. We said they didn't. Where did they stop to eat? They didn't. We explained they ate and slept on the rocket. In describing it, we told her it was very small. She asked if it had a bathroom. We said no to which she said "a ha…then where do they go to the bathroom?"

She was convinced she'd caught us. If there was no bathroom and it took a few days…then they couldn't be on the moon…nobody can hold it that long. Besides what's up there when they arrive…nothing…still no place to go to the bathroom." She wasn't well educated…but she wasn't stupid. Until the day she died, she was convinced there were tiny people in the television.

By the time I finished high school I had become addicted to television. But unlike most kids, I watched a lot of news & talk shows. I would watch the *American Farmer* at 6:00 a.m., the *Today Show*, Walter Cronkite, Steve Allen and Jack Parr.

I couldn't imagine anything better than being on TV. However, it never occurred to me that I would be on television, at least not without getting arrested!

In 1974, at age 24 I wrote a letter to a local TV station criticizing their noon talk show. *Danny's Day* was an institution in Oklahoma City. Host Danny Williams was a one-man army who dominated local radio and television. For some reason I thought I could give Danny advice. I wrote him a letter saying he needed more business news to make his show a success.

Now, this guy was the hottest thing on Oklahoma City TV, and I was going to give him advice. The closest I've ever gotten to television was to change the channel.

It's Not Intelligent Vision

Danny was kind enough to invite me on his show to talk about how to shop. At the time I was teaching school at a local junior college. I knew a little about economics and money and tried to relate it to buying cars, houses, appliances and what have you.

Prepared to speak for about 30 minutes, I went to the station to do the show. Danny advised me I'd have three minutes. Somehow he didn't see me being the entire program. Anyway, I did the show and after my three minutes were up, I stood in the wings watching, mesmerized by live television.

When the show ended, Danny came over, said good job, and asked me if I could speak about something next week. I said sure (having no idea what it would be) and Danny invited me back.

That very good fortune, and the guidance of Danny Williams helped me build a career in television. I did *Danny's Day* every week for a year. When one of the other stations in town started a morning news program, they invited me to be on their show as well.

Lola Hall was another TV giant in Oklahoma City at that time. Lola said she'd like me to do business news but the station couldn't pay much. Hell, I was working for free on *Danny's Day*. I was thinking I'd do this if I had to pay them. I would end up doing both shows simultaneously.

After two years with Danny (for free) and one year with Lola for about $10 a show, I approached Danny's boss about being paid. He said no. I said they paid me at the other station and he said "To do what?"

I had been doing the news on the competing station, for a year and he still didn't know. He advised me there was no way I could keep appearing on both stations. I called his bluff and he finally agreed to pay me about $100 a month. To hear him tell it the station might have to sell their building to afford me. To me another $1,200 a year was a 20% raise on my then $6,000 a year teaching salary.

About one year later Tom Kirby, a man who has since become one of the most innovative newsmen in the country, recruited me to the third station in town. When he approached me, he asked what I was being paid by the station. As much as $1,200 meant to me, I felt like a fool telling him that was all they paid me. He said look; I'm not getting into a bidding war. We'll pay you $18,000 a year. That's it. It was all I could do not to wet my pants, but I said I'd think about it and let him know.

He said he wanted an answer now. I hesitated because I was afraid he'd find out they were only paying me $1,200 a year. He took my hesitation as negotiating and said look I'll go as high as $25,000 but I want an answer now.

I said yes, signed a contract the next day and never looked back. A few months later, Kirby called me into his office.

Kirby:　"Hey Orza, you're gonna anchor tonight."

Now I didn't know the first thing about anchoring, but Kirby briefed me and I stumbled through the news as a substitute. Just before I went on the air, Kirby grabbed me and said:

"We gotta change your name."

Now this caught me by surprise. I had been Vinny Orza for 28 years.

Kirby:　"As of tonight you're Vince."

Vince:　"Why?"

Kirby:　"Because you can't say good evening, twelve people were killed today, I'm Vinny Orza. It will sound like you did it."

From that day on, I was Vince Orza. KOCO/TV in Oklahoma City gave me the privilege and honor of reporting and anchoring for them for almost twelve years. I would do the news every night while teaching marketing every morning at the University. To me television was just like teaching, only with a larger classroom. The best part was my students were wonderful critics of what and how I did. Being a newsman made me something of a celebrity in my family. Years later my cousins would tell me how their parents were so proud that an Orza had made the "big time," but it wasn't always so big time.

In television news you are often advised to ignore the inevitable verbal fumble, fly on your nose, or loud background noise. In spite of how bad it may be in the studio, the audience at home is often totally unaware of what's going on. I say often because some things just can't be hidden. Like the night I was anchoring and kidding around with our weather guy Wayne Shattuck. We were in a commercial break and somehow we both started speaking like the cartoon character Elmer Fudd. The cameraman cued me, so I straightened my tie and cuffs, looked straight in the camera as he counted me down to the end of the commercial.

Cameraman: "3...2...1... you're on."

    Vince: "In other news tonight, President Wonald
             Weagan said."

I found myself thinking, excuse me, did I just say President Wonald Weagan? I could hear Wayne choking back a giant laugh. As I finished my story, I turned to speak with Wayne about the weather and choosing my words and letters very carefully and deliberately I said:

    "Well Wayne...how is the weather?"

Wayne smiled ear-to-ear and said:

    "Oh it's weally gonna wain."

The only thing worse than a few hundred thousand people hearing you say Wonald Weagan is going into a class to teach sixty students the next morning and having them greet you with:

    "Wonald Weagan?"

"Never get into fights with ugly people because they have nothing to lose."
- Unknown

19 Insanity Is Hereditary, You Get It From Your Kids

"Give your child a spanking once a day, Even if you don't know why they will."

- Sam Levenson

The moment I became a parent I learned that God has a sense of humor. I'm convinced God made kids as a joke to play on parents. Sam Levenson was a wonderful old Jewish comic I used to watch on the Ed Sullivan Show. He said it best. "Insanity is hereditary, you get it from your kids."

Perhaps Bill Cosby performed the best description of the process of birth years ago. Cosby described the obstetrician sitting there positioned between the woman's legs like a baseball catcher waiting for the baby to arrive.

I watched the births of both my daughters. Now, I'm pretty well educated, yet I still don't see how this works. First of all, the baby doesn't fit. Honest, I defy anyone to fold that kid up and get it back inside. Impossible...it's just too large.

Secondly, we humans generate millions of babies a year with incredible quality control. Oh, sure we occasionally have children with defects, yet invariably we over compensate for one short fall by enhancing performance in some other area. Why can't car companies do this? When you get a car that's a lemon, the whole thing's a mistake. Having taught school, I'm convinced no human is a total lemon. My best students were often confined to wheelchairs or unable to speak, but they were brilliant. Babies born without all their limbs, with learning deficiencies, with enormous medical problems are still wonderful gifts from God. But a lousy car has no redeeming value.

My job, by the way, during the birth of my children went far beyond the normal breathing coach. For our kids, I was responsible for wiping sweat and to do color commentary during the play-by-play. I, after all, had been a television news anchor.

Vince: "Okay, they're bringing over all the tools."

Cosby called them salad spoons.

Patti: "Ask them to move that mirror so I can see."

I couldn't believe my wife was that strong. To watch your own pain is real strength.

Vince: "Okay, okay, okay, okay."

Patti: "Okay, what?"

Vince: "Okay, okay, okay."

Patti: "Can you see if it's a boy or a girl?"

Vince: "Oh my God!"

Patti: "What? What's wrong?"

Vince: "Okay...its got dark hair."

My wife is French, German, Bohemian...a virtual mixed bag of fair-skinned and light-haired cultures. I'm Italian (pure Italian), olive skin, brown hair. Dark hair meant I could chalk one up for the Italians and our dominant coloring.

Patti: "But is it a boy or girl with dark hair?"

Patti is always worried about technicalities.

Vince: "It's a girl."

Chalk one up for fair-skinned mixed breeds.

Patti and I have two terrific daughters. Both teenagers, they are also proof the apple doesn't fall far from the tree. Patti has wonderful memories of growing up, including the times she spent with her grandmother. It is a tradition Patti passed along to our girls, who just like Patti enjoy spending the weekend with their grandmother. Patti's grandmother taught her to play cards and guess what, Patti and her mother taught our girls to play cards. There are "grandmother" activities, "grandmother" foods, and events that can only occur with "grandmother."

By the way I suspect my family is no different than most. We have "Grandmother" (Patti's mom) and "Grandma" (my mom). Although we face the same dilemma many other families face; being uncles and aunts that live a long way away, we try our best to keep the kids in contact with their cousins. Landi and Alix always looked up to Patti's brother's older daughters. Likewise, our girls get a kick out of being the older cousins to Patti's sister's boys. I can't help but believe much of those feelings come from the stories we told them about being with our cousins when we were kids.

I'm also convinced being with family teaches us to want to have family. Hence, I was pleased when Landi started having her own family, even if it was at the age of four. Remember the Care Bear craze a few years back? Well Landi has a collection of them. One day when I came home from work, I walked in the den only to find Landi and her "children" watching TV. There she was with about two-dozen Care Bears sitting on the couch lined up in size order watching TV. She was insistent her "children" share their imaginary tea and cookies and be well behaved as they watched cartoons. If they did step out of line Landi would say, "Do you want a spanking?" Pop continues to remind me the apple doesn't fall too far from the tree.

Kids who grow up without families miss the learning that comes with being around others who share values, stories, foods and traditions. Immigrants fast figured out that the more experiences their children had, the better they would fit into their new society. In that vein, my folks allowed and encouraged me to do many more things than was common. Likewise, Patti and I want so much more for our girls, we allow and encourage them to have as many life and family experiences as possible.

We've sent the girls to camp, taken them on trips across the nation and around the world. They've flown in airplanes, ridden trains, subways, and hot air balloons, cruised the oceans and down the Nile River. While we have taken them to Disney World, we are more inclined to have them see the Grand Canyon or Yellowstone. To us, family trips are more education and experiences than entertainment. It seems to me that all too many American families are satisfied with trips to Disney World, Universal Studios and Hard Rock Cafe or Planet Hollywood restaurants as a great family outing. Those things are fine, but I don't believe they provide any long-term social value.

Vacations are expensive, but it costs more to spend a week at Disney World or Universal Studios than it does in Europe. My grandparents taught my folks, who taught me, that life is a matter of choices. We can't have and can't afford everything we want. Traveling takes money, but it also takes sacrifice. I was taught to save money and I've taught my girls to save. All those lessons in "no waste" result in extra dollars to save and spend on trips. We don't waste money smoking cigarettes (do the math and you'll see a pack a day is at least one plane ticket a year).

We believe books; library cards and reading are better and less expensive than video games. Our kids bring a lunch to school rather than eating in the cafeteria. It's not only cheaper - it's better! We don't buy our girls' faddish clothes or every "hot" toy and, in spite of the fact I work in the restaurant business, we don't eat out as often as is common today. Why? Because it's expensive and we'd rather use our money to travel. Think of it this way. If you spend $10-$15 a day on food away from home (which is probably a lot less than the typical family of four) you are spending about $5,000 a year. That's the equivalent of two family vacations. Using our logic, we still get to eat everyday; we just do it at home or by bringing a meal from home, plus go on vacation.

When we travel, we want the girls to experience different things. We encourage the girls to say please, thank you, hello, and goodbye in the language of the land we are visiting. Like my grandparents, I believe we should fit in to the society we are visiting, rather than stand out. We eat native and visit as many local sites as possible. When they were small, we'd also visit a local zoo or animal park as the reward for being well behaved. Thus our girls have been to zoos across Europe, the U.S. and Mexico.

When I was a kid we took family trips to Florida. We drove straight through to save the cost of a motel. Just in case we had car trouble, my mother packed enough food to last five days. We stopped along side of the road, had picnics, used gas station restrooms and bought few, if any, souvenirs. Our money was spent getting there, being there and coming home.

Patti and I do the same things with our girls. While times have changed a little since I was a kid, adventures are similar. We started taking our girls on longer vacations when they were only three and five years old. Friends would voice concern about taking the girls on long flights. Not to worry, Patti would pack those cards. Remember learning to play cards with Grandmother? Well, it came in handy while flying. The girls brought coloring books, books to read and puzzles and stuffed animals to play with. They also learned a trick from their mom. Bring your own pillow. It's easier to sleep when you're comfortable.

Our oldest daughter, Landi, collects everything. She's got ticket stubs, pictures and post cards from every place we've visited. When Patti and I traveled without the girls, we always brought them back a doll. Landi has a huge collection of dolls from across the world. Alix has a similar collection, only two years less of it. Alix likes wearing hats and has a neat collection of them from across the world. We also would bring back traditional native clothing from places we visited. The girls have wonderful Spanish dresses, Middle Eastern robes, wooden shoes from Holland, Mexican hats and countless other items that help them remember where they have been or want to go if we traveled without them.

A few years ago we cruised the Baltic's, Scandinavian countries and into Russia. The ship was small and elegant. We dressed up for dinner each evening. Among other things, the girls learned about formal dining, artistic napkin folding and seven course dinners. In each country we visited, the girls added to their collection of dolls and foreign clothing. The sightseeing was outstanding; the girls even had a chance to visit the palace in St. Petersburg where Rasputin was killed. At the theater in the palace, we were treated to a Russian ballet, piano and opera recital and concert of instruments native to Russia. The girls knew it was an experience few, if any, of her other friends would ever have...even at the Russian pavilion at Disney World.

A few weeks after we came home, Landi announced she had a surprise for us. Impressed by the formal dining on board the ship, she wanted to provide a similar dining experience for Patti and me at home. Dress would be formal! That evening we were treated to a table setting fit for the palace dining room. Napkins folded as they were on the ship, candlelight, white wine chilled, and red wine at room temperature. She had created and printed a menu for the "Cafe Landi." She called my mother (grandma vs. grandmother) and got instructions on how to prepare several foods that were my favorites. She had arranged to have one of her former teachers, who was something of a big sister to her, take her shopping for the ingredients. Even more amazingly, she prepared, served and coordinated a wonderful dinner of appetizer, soup, salad, entree, dessert, fruit, nuts, coffee and my favorite, strawberries and Grand Marnier.

I could not have been more proud of my daughter. A vacation grew to become more than just sightseeing. It had become an education and still another experience to add to our list of family activities. No parents bringing their kids' home from Disney World received a similar reward from their children. At a time when many families can't get their kids to help around the house or in the kitchen, my daughter volunteered to feed us like we were royalty! And, yes, she even cleaned up. When the apple falls close to the tree, sometimes its seeds grow to become an even better tree.

"The first sign of maturity is the discovery that the volume knob also turns to the left."
- "Smile" Zingers

20 Our Girls

"Motivation is like bathing - it may not last, but it's still a good idea now and then."

- Jim Cathcart

God knew what he/she was doing when he/she created kids. Being a parent is more fun than anything else on the face of the earth.

Art Linkletter made a fortune with his books, "Kids Say the Darndest Things." Art was right.

I always tease Patti about money. She can't win. I either complain she spends too much or not enough. When she's frugal, I call her a cheapskate. When our youngest daughter, Alix, heard me call Patti a cheapskate, she began to use the phrase as well. Well, almost. Alix would look at me while teasing her mom and with a big smile and strong sense of confidence, tell Patti, "Mommy, you're a cheesecake."

When I was a kid, Pop and my uncles used money to talk us into doing what they wanted. At Thanksgiving, we got a dollar for eating a whole turkey drumstick. As a parent, I have also used money to make my kids do certain things.

A few years ago, our girls learned how to turn the lights on. Obviously this is not a major accomplishment. The major accomplishment is teaching them to turn them off, which my girls could not master. Hence, I decided to invoke the penalty of a 25¢ fine for leaving the lights on in their rooms.

Alix paid for one of my trips to Europe that year! Whenever I came home from work and found a light on, I'd holler, "Alix." By the third or fourth time I'd done this she knew what she'd done wrong. So when I came in and yelled, she'd instantly run to her room, turn off the light, get a quarter from her piggy bank and run back to me, give me a hello kiss and a quarter.

One day I came home and yelled, "Alix." She shot to her room, turned off the light, grabbed her money, came back to see me, gave me a kiss and 30¢

Vince: "Alix, what's the 30¢ for?"

Alix: "Daddy, the 25¢ is for leaving the light on."

Vince: "Yes, but what's the nickel for?"

Alix: "Daddy, you really do a good job helping me turn the lights off, so I gave you a bonus."

I've taught my kids to understand the value of a job well done!

Patti and I also have taught the girls to be responsible for themselves. Cleaning their rooms, flushing the toilet, turning off the lights, straightening up their closet and making the bed are S.O.P. at the Orza house.

My parents laid down the same rules for me. When I was a kid I never left my room without making my bed, but Alix went me one better.

I don't sleep very much. I'm up most nights reading or watching TV. Alix has my sleep habits or actually, lack of sleep habits. One night about 3:00 a.m., Alix came down to the den to watch TV with me. After a few minutes, I suggested that Alix and I go back to bed. When I carried her into her room I learned how well trained she was. Her bed was already made.

Kids really do say and do the darndest things. The highlight of my day is coming home from work to a great kiss and hug and words, "Hi, Daddy" and the goodnight kiss and hugs and words, "I love you, Daddy." "I love you too, girls.

Older parents tell me the feeling never changes any no matter how old either party gets.

"Everyone is in awe of the lion tamer in a cage with half a dozen lions - everyone but a school bus driver."

- Unknown

21 Pop's Logic

"You write me that it will be impossible...the word is not French."

- Napoleon

My folks gave me a few simple ground rules for life. My father always said to me that it's okay to fail. It means you tried. You learn more from reading and listening than speaking. People can be different, can believe different things, eat different foods, worship different Gods and be different colors and it's good that they are, otherwise life would be boring.

Save. Don't waste. Clean up after yourself, remember you are no better than anyone else is and remember your roots.

If life were easy, everyone would be rich and happy. Life isn't easy but it's worth all of your efforts. Being a kid is tough; being a parent is tougher. Tragedy strikes but life goes on.

Rule #12: You don't get everything you want in life and you don't want everything you get.

My folks live a few miles from me in Edmond, Oklahoma. Out of all the logic and common sense passed among our family, perhaps the best is the simplest.

My folks always let me know I could tell them anything. No matter what the problem, the circumstances or who's involved my parents let me know, "We're your parents, you can trust us." They may not agree, may think me a damn fool, may advise against, but they want to know "You can depend on us...we're your parents...you can depend on family." The love my parents gave me taught me what kind of father to be to my girls.

When I went to Oklahoma to attend college, my dad expected I would return to New York to work in the family business he had started three decades prior. Pop and his two brothers were self-made men. Pop expected me to be one as well but I think it surprised him when I decided to remain in Oklahoma.

My family never quite knew where Oklahoma was. Like most New Yorkers, they could see about as far west as Pittsburgh. Then they thought there was a giant desert, with Las Vegas at the end followed by California. One time while I was home for spring break, my Uncle Ed called me over to introduce me to a customer. This is my nephew Vinny. He goes to school in Okinawa. I said "Uncle Ed, its Oklahoma." He said "Oklahoma, Okinawa...whatever.

All of my uncles and aunts lived in the Bronx. For the most part, they had never left the Bronx other than to venture up to our house in Connecticut or vacation in the Catskill Mountains of New York. To them Oklahoma was another country. They knew we had Indians and I think they expected I was surrounded by reservations, needed the pony express to get the mail and used horses to get to work at the fort!

In a way, my dad was a pioneer, the first member of his family to move away. In the 1940's, moving to Connecticut was like moving to Oklahoma. Thus, no one was surprised when I moved to Oklahoma permanently. Pop asked me two or three more times if I wanted his part of the family business. I said no, so he and Mom retired to Florida, once again leaving the family behind. Years later other members of the family would retire to Florida as well but Pop led the way.

A few years after Patti and I were married and began our family, I asked Pop and Mom to move to Oklahoma. "What are we going to do there?" I knew there were two things I could say that would make the move happen. "I need your help at the business (the one I had started, the apple doesn't fall too far from the tree) and that I wanted the girls to have their grandparents close by." That was it. They sold their house in Florida and moved to Oklahoma. My girls have had the benefit of having Patti's mom and my parents close by. We've shared stories, traditions and memories. They will be better for the time and experiences they've had with their grandparents. More important, they will have stories, a culture and traditions to pass along to their children.

The world would be a better place if more kids had families, traditions, uncles, aunts, cousins, grandparents and the stories of life as part of their everyday existence.

Some people do a terrific job raising their kids with only one parent around. Some grandparents do the job for parents unwilling or unable. Growing up with family, any size, any color, any religion is better than growing up in a day care center. There's nothing wrong with day care, but you can't pay people to love your kids. Sure they can teach them and often day care is the only alternative, but it is no substitute for family.

Hilary Clinton wrote a book a few years back called *It Takes a Village*. Sadly, politics made the book controversial. Its message was simple. Kids need help growing up. Some of us are lucky enough to have families'…big families, with aunts, uncles, cousins, grandparents and two parents. For those not so fortunate, a village, or neighbors or anyone else that cares is better than growing up lonely and without direction.

When I was a kid, everyone knew everyone else in the neighborhood. Not so much that people were buddy-buddy. Rather, it was a matter of being neighborly. People watched out for each other and each other's kids. When grandparents lived with you or next door, they would sit outside watching the traffic, the kids playing and shoot the breeze with everyone and anyone that walked by. We talked to and learned from our grandparents and everyone else's. We learned to respect our elders and go to them for guidance. Oklahoma Indians called them "wise men."

Families today, are spread across the nation. Many kids never know their aunts, uncles, cousins, grandparents or even the neighbors. Today Wal-Mart hires people to be friendly. Have you ever noticed the older man or woman who greets you when you walk into Wal-Mart? They are paid to be friendly. It's a nice gesture, but something is wrong when there aren't enough people around to be friendly for free!

Family doesn't have to be a blood relationship.

Some people are lucky enough to become family by being in close proximity. Pop is a surrogate father to several people we work with. Friends whose fathers have died or abandoned them call my father Pop and come to him for advice or just for a shoulder to cry on. Likewise, my mother and father are always on the look out for that stray person who may be looking for a little extra family time. When they moved to Oklahoma, they were lucky enough to buy a house with great neighbors, one of who refers to himself as the third son. My folks appreciate that and the third son appreciates Mom and Pop.

The world would be a much better place if more kids had parents and grandparents like mine. The wit, wisdom, patience, impatience, commitment, dedication, traditions, logic and common sense you get from your elders and loved ones make you a better person. My mom and dad believe in the American dream and taught me to as well.

One final bit of immigrant logic:

Rule #13: **Believe in the American dream, yourself, the future, family, and believe in God. If you do, everything is possible.**

"Leaders are made, usually self-made."
- Warren Bennis

Epilogue...

or as New Yorker's say..."An a nudder ting..."

"Those who weep recover more quickly than those who smile."

Jean Giraudoux

When I sat down to write my book I wanted nothing more than to give people a light hearted look at life. I have been very gratified by the letters, comments, emails, and phone calls I have received from people telling me how much they enjoyed my stories and how the book helped them stop and think about what was really important in life. When I was a kid growing up in Connecticut, I only knew what I knew. The beauty of being a child is you are optimistic about everything. You believe in Santa Claus and the Easter Bunny, you are spell bound by the fireworks on the Fourth of July. If you are lucky enough to have wonderful parents, (which I did), you think everyone has great parents...because you only know what you know.

As you grow older, you begin to realize how much you don't know. You begin to realize that life can be dangerous, things happen without warning, bad things happen to good people, about divorce, disease, death, tragedy, bad luck and a host of things that happen everyday to people who are just trying to get by. Slowly the optimism of childhood gives way to the cynicism of adulthood. It's starts out simply enough with a friend doing something that disappoints you, a parent loses a job, you get dumped by a boyfriend or girlfriend, get poor grades on a test after studying all night convinced you would do well. It seems the older you get the worse the day-to-day bad news can get. A spouse, parent, friend or, worst of all, a child dies. Someone you love is attacked, raped or killed. Let's face it. As great as any day can be it can be ten times worse when things are going terribly wrong.

When I hear politicians talk about 'family values', I want to throw up. It's politics at its worst. Political campaigns are all too often filthy with lies and misrepresentations...a kind of political pornography. Candidates seem to say and do anything to get themselves elected. Then once they get in office, they start preaching about family values. It's hypocritical but it works. Individuals claiming to be devout Christians have orchestrated some of the nastiest campaigns. And we're supposed to take advice from them on how to live our lives. Life is really pretty simple. No one is a saint, everyone commits sins, and each of us has done things, which in retrospect we probably wouldn't do again. That's part of being human. The good news is most of us don't have our stupid moments detailed on the front page of the paper every day. In fact, that's what keeps so many very good and qualified people from getting involved in the political system. And thankfully, many of us have families, who unlike political foes, forgive us our sins.

That's why it's so important to have great family and friends. I have been fortunate enough to travel across the U.S. and around a good part of the world. The more I traveled and met people of different races, colors and creeds, different ethnic backgrounds, different political persuasions, the more I realized how similar we all are. If you are a parent, no religious, political or ethnic belief will make you love your kids more or less. Ethnicity has nothing to do with it. The bond between parent and child is universal. The bond between child and parent, no matter the age of either is universal. Laughter is universal and so are tears. Friends can become enemies and enemies can become friends. Perhaps this is the most wonderful thing about the United States. People from every corner of the globe have moved here and despite their prejudices, biases, historical battles, they learn to get along with each other because they have become Americans. In two hundred years, our nation and its people have overcome the divisions people living in the countries we have all emigrated from still fight today.

To that end, it's becoming almost impossible to take an American census that identifies someone's racial and ethnic roots. I say I'm Italian. Both of my parents' families came from around Naples, Italy. Well on a Mediterranean Cruise a few years back, I learned the French and Spanish controlled Naples for a few hundred years. Better yet, while sightseeing in Monaco, we visited the palace and found my mothers maiden name on the family tree of the royal family. By the way, the royal family of Monaco are descendants of Napoleon. So what am I - Italian, French and Spanish? And the Moors (who were mostly Muslims) controlled Spain for a few hundred years. So what if one of my perhaps Spanish great, great, great, great grandfathers had a Moor for a wife? And my other great, great, great grandmother hung around some of those Frenchmen, who lived on the border of Germany, who were sailors and traveled to the Greek Islands? Now what am I? What's worse, my wife is part Bohemian, (which doesn't even exist as a country anymore...and when it did it had a lot of Gypsies!!!), is also part French and German and God knows what else. So this makes our kids walking examples of the United Nations!

Now here's where it gets really dicey. What if they marry the son of the Jewish doctor whose family emigrated from Russia who married the North African woman whose family worked the mines for the Dutch in South Africa?

That's the beauty of America. There really aren't any pure Americans. Our diversity is our strength. And our families are the beneficiaries of that diversity. So if nothing else, I hope my book helped you realize how and why you should embrace your family. For all their flaws, scars, the aggravation and pain they may cause, they also offer a heritage that helped make you what you are. Like I said earlier, family doesn't have to be by blood. Great friends often become better family than the ones born to you.

I have a great family by blood and by way of friends. What follows are the final chapters of one part of my family story. I hope you see how difficult losing that family can be. I've come to the conclusion that my generation of adults is not doing a very good job preparing our children or ourselves for the inevitable in life. When I was a kid and an uncle, aunt, neighbor or someone of importance to our family died, I and all the other kids in our family attended the funerals with our parents. It was how they taught us to sit quietly in church, to understand that life begins and ends. I can remember the first time I touched the skin of someone dead...the cold, waxy feel of what I previously had known as warm and loving. Strangely enough, it was how we learned about life. The funeral taught us about coming together in much the same way as weddings, first communions, sweet-sixteen parties for the girls and anniversary parties for grandparents taught us about life. A feast follows a funeral (at the home of the deceased)...because there is no event for which Italians can't figure a reason to eat.

The assemblies of family and friends were always a lot of fun. There were stories and reminiscing, children of all ages running around the house and the transference of memories of those who had passed on. It's the stuff from which traditions are made. As a result of all those occasions, I'm comfortable attending funerals. Sure there is sorrow and pain, but looking back while seeing the children that provide hope for the future make it all come together. Once again, you only know what you know; I never realized how many families shelter their children from funerals. As a result, all too many adults can't handle the death of a loved one. In many cases, they grow to adulthood without ever attending a funeral. Even worse, they aren't very well prepared to deal with the closing days and months of life for those we love that are sick or elderly.

After my father died, I decided to add an epilogue and few additional final chapters to my book. I don't want it to be maudlin rather I hope it will give you some insight as to what you can expect and how to endure the pain of death for someone you love. Indeed, I hope it helps you realize how to really enjoy the closing moments of life with the people you love. Pop's death was slow and miserable, yet in spite of that, we had moments that were funny, touching, enjoyable, hopefully and most of all with an ever-increasing awareness of how much we all loved each other. His death brought me closer to my sister and brother while teaching me to be a better husband and father to Patti and the girls. It also taught how wonderful a wife and daughter-in-law Patti really was. This more than anything else may be the most important thing my father ever gave or taught me.

So get a box of tissues and read on. If I've done my job correctly, these final chapters will help you increase your appreciation for your family.

To weep is to make less the depth of grief.

Shakespeare

22 Oklahoma Angels

"I have miles to go before I sleep."

- Robert Frost

MY FATHER DIED...

No matter how prepared we think we are for death, we're not prepared. Just saying the words "my father died" chokes me up. In spite of the fact I knew I would someday have to say those words, I never really knew how difficult it would be. Pop passed away just as millions of other men and women...a victim of cancer.

A smoker all of his life, he never could quit. Mark Twain said he never could understand all the talk about how difficult it was to quit smoking. "Hell it ain't hard, I must've done it a thousand times." Pop was Mark Twain...he knew he should quit, tried to quit, but couldn't overcome the urge for another cigarette.

Years ago he stopped smoking in front of me. Not out of respect, fear or concern. He stopped smoking in front of me because he was tired of hearing me complain about it. Actually, I think he stopped smoking around my family because Patti told him she wouldn't let him be around the girls smelling of smoke. It's amazing what grandparents will do for their grandchildren, that they would never consider doing for their own kids. I'm of the opinion God figured this out and created grand children to keep old people in line!

Pop died on July 20, 2000. Diagnosed with cancer for the second time in his life, this time in his throat, it was the cruelest of all possibilities. It meant he would lose his ability to eat. As Italians, the only thing more important than food is family; and family without food is impossible. Eating is why we come together.

He started having trouble swallowing in the fall of 1999. We finally got him to see a doctor who sent him to the hospital for some tests. The results were everything we feared. Having said that, the last eight months of my father's life brought us a whole new group of people who would become "part of the family."

The first of God's Oklahoma saints was a doctor by the name of John Randolph. Recognized as one of the "areas finest surgeons," Randolph has one of the best bedside manners anywhere. John Randolph was the one who broke the news to us about Pop's cancer. In fact, true to our Italian life style, I met with Randolph prior to his examination of my father and told him I wanted to know the results before he told Pop. John let me know that wasn't how it worked; his first responsibility was to the patient.

I explained to him that my father had passed the torch to me, and as head of the family, it was my responsibility to deliver the news. Prior to coming to the hospital for the tests, my father and I had a long hard discussion of what he wanted in the event the news wasn't good. I had my marching orders from Pop. He told me he trusted me to make the right decision for him, believing I would better understand the situation. It took a lot of persuading to convince Randolph to tell me my father was dying. I can't say I was surprised by the news, but it still hit me like a ton of bricks. Randolph discussed the options with me. We could have chemo, radiation, surgery, or do nothing. No matter what the choice, at age 83, my father's options were not very encouraging, but John Randolph provided a wonderful mix of optimism and encouragement. He explained that while it wasn't good it wasn't necessarily an immediate death sentence. I asked him what he recommended with one simple question.

"John...if this was your father what would you do?"

His eyes welled up with a hint of tears as he explained to me that his father passed away recently and that he too had faced this kind of decision.

"John...my father doesn't want to go through this to be a vegetable. If he is not going to be able to walk out of here and play golf again, then let's not waste the time and money." Randolph told me he could and would get my father through this.

We walked in to speak with Pop. My father knew in an instant that the news was not good. He reached out to hold my hand, squeezing as he said to Randolph, "What's the story Doc? Give it to me straight." Randolph explained the situation and said he believed surgery was the correct decision. True to his word, my father looked at me and asked me the toughest question of my life. "What do you think Bub?" Within a few short minutes of meeting with John Randolph, I had developed a respect and admiration for him. More importantly, it was apparent my father liked him and we both trusted him. So I told my father John was the doctor and we should go for the surgery.

Pop's response was short and sweet. "Ok…when? Let's not waste any time. I want to be back playing golf by spring."

Randolph never flinched. "I'll have you and your son out playing golf by spring."

Pop asked me to tell my mother the news. I think the thing that worried my father the most was how my mother would handle the news. They had lived virtually every moment of their lives together for nearly seven decades. He took care of her and the family, all of the bills, all of the decisions. She took care of the children, home and made sure everyone was happy and healthy. Pop was worried about her being alone. Randolph helped explain to my mother what he was going to do. He went out of his way to give my mother the confidence she needed to place the life of her husband of 62 years in his hands.

John Randolph performed the surgery on my father a few days later. Randolph was thoughtful enough to send his nurse out during the surgery to tell us that Pop was doing well. A few hours later, John came out to tell us everything had gone very well, that Pop had come through the procedure like a man half his 83 years of age. Once again, Randolph's bedside manner made all the difference in the world.

Pop came through the operation with flying colors. However, his recovery was marred by pneumonia and a few other mishaps that resulted in him spending weeks in intensive care and nearly three months in the hospital. The man I brought home from the hospital weighed nearly 60 pounds less than the man I brought to the hospital. While he was there, he grew very fond of Kathy Tagnesi, the Vice President of Administration, and Kay Mallory one of the nurses that cared for him in the rehab center. These two women took care of my father as though he was their dad. There are no words to say thank you enough for the love, affection and care any of these people provided Pop.

Little did any of us know how difficult the next few month would be. Our faith and trust in John Randolph turned out to well placed. He told me to call him anytime of the day or n gave me all of his phone numbers and never failed to retu calls - sometimes at two or three o'clock in the morning after having completed several hours of surgery on other patients. He would always apologize for calling so late. The apologies were unnecessary given the fact he had so many other patients and issues to address. If Randolph treated all of his patients the way he treated Pop, he could be the poster child for great medicine!

Pop's recovery was slow, and over the months that followed, he regained some strength but not his weight. He looked weak and frail and was wobbly on his feet. Worst of all, the surgery did not cure the problem. A few months after the surgery to remove the growth on Pop's esophagus, the cancer was back. Pop wound up in the same condition he had been in prior to the surgery, unable to swallow. A tube was inserted in his stomach and he was taking all his nourishment through it. It was cruelest of all possible fates...Pop was unable to eat.

But...on a pretty spring day in early April, Pop and I mounted a cart to play some golf. It wasn't the game we usually enjoyed; but he chipped a few shots, sank a couple of putts and watched me play. I purposefully walked away from the cart so as not to let Pop see me crying as I watched the man I loved live out what we both knew were the closing days of his life.

Yesterday is history,

Tomorrow is a mystery.

Today is a gift from God...

That's why we call it
the present.

23 The Surgery

> "You must be the change you wish to see in the world."
>
> - Mahatma Ghandi

I started making notes about my mother and father the night I met John Randolph. I knew that no matter how prepared I was for the eventual death of my dad; I was not prepared. The night before Pop's surgery I lay in bed knowing no matter the genius of John Randolph or any of the doctors, at age 83, Pop's best years were behind him. I awoke at 5 a.m. and laid in the dark crying almost uncontrollably.

When I arrived at the hospital the morning of Pop's surgery he had on his best game face. He thanked me for being there and began to tell me what he would say to me almost daily for the rest of his life. The words were wonderful but gave me a mix of pain and pleasure…"I'm so proud of you," he would tell me. To this day I have flashbacks of Pop lying in his hospital bed telling me he was proud of me.

Likewise, I had the luxury of telling my dad how much I loved him and how great a father he was to me. In that respect, we were both much luckier than those who lose someone quickly. We had the time to say thank you, I love you, and goodbye. We also had the time to discuss his final wishes.

As we waited for them to come and take him to surgery, we talked about playing golf. "I'm walking out of here on my own," he told me. "I know Pop…we'll play golf together again." And then the orderlies came to take him down to surgery. It was the first time I ever remember seeing fear in my father's eyes. He looked at me, both of us fighting back tears but our eyes watering almost beyond control. Prior to surgery, my mother, wife and daughters visited with Pop to wish him good luck and tell them they loved him. Pop tried to be strong and it was family at its best. Everyone offering hope, love and strength.

During his surgery I could not help but reflect back on all I shared with my parents over the 50 years of my life. My parents were depression era people. The older I get, the more I realize how much I have become my parents. They absolutely refused to waste anything. Their home, and to some degree mine, are collections of things we simply can't bring ourselves to throw away. The hotel soaps, shampoos and creams are only the tip of the iceberg. We saved bottles, jars so as not to use store bought plastic bags, scraps of fabric my mother would sew together into ironing board covers, pillows and whatever else she could dream up. We had little bottles of liquor from the airlines, old magazines, old clothing…junk to others, personal possessions to those who successfully traversed the dark days of the 20th century.

I sat there thinking about my parents coming for dinner at our home, always entering through the garage. The garage entrance led directly to the kitchen, which to my parents symbolized family. The front door was for guests. In fact, Pop was fond of saying, "The first time you're a guest, after that you're a pest."

We often ate together two or three times per week. When we arrived at their home, we too entered through the garage. There in the kitchen were my parents, Pop sitting at the counter supervising my mother making dinner. If he wasn't in the kitchen, he was napping in front of the television.

In the last days of his life, Pop would sit at the counter or in his chair too weak to get up. But he would give us a little flick of the wrist as his sign of welcome or goodbye. As we would bend down to kiss him hello or goodbye, he would stretch up to place his lips on our cheeks and hoarsely whisper, "I love you" to each of us.

I found myself thinking of Pop's garage, his workbench full of tools for a man who could fix anything. That depression era mentality led his generation of men and women to be self-sufficient and so no matter the task he could handle it himself. The garage also held a collection of things Pop saved. Scattered throughout were golf clubs, remnants of his wood burning hobby and his golf trophies. In their younger days, he and my mother had won the husband and wife tournament, what he called the "divorce tournament." Pop had been club champion. A natural jock, as a kid he had played ball against Babe Ruth. The garage also held a refrigerator/freezer always fully stocked with samples of steaks, coffee, chicken, cakes and every other imaginable food he snagged from my office. It pained them to see food being wasted. My parents always had enough food on hand to last for months or feed anyone who might drop in unannounced. Should another depression ever occur, they were prepared. Those of us who never lived through the great depression would do well to learn how precious food could be.

Indeed, my parents never came for dinner without bringing something with them. The items they brought all had special significance. My mother would always bake a loaf of Italian bread...the communion of life. She would occasionally bring fruit, homemade jelly, an eggplant, a strange gift, but one that had an extra special significance since Patti grew to love eggplant parmesan on her first trip to meet my parents 20 years before. It was their way of saying, "we love you" to Patti. On really important occasions, my mother would bring Patti and the girls, doilies she had crocheted. All were simple and loving gifts of family.

During the hours of surgery, I realized I was reliving the life my parents had given me. Only then did I understand how much more we lose when a life ends. I sat there looking at my 86-year-old mother. I grew up watching "Leave It To Beaver," recognizing I did not live with Ward and June Cleaver, but our life was just as idealistic, just as full of lessons on right and wrong, good and bad, and most important...just as happy.

I stared at the wrinkles in Mom's face, neck and hands. As I looked at her, I closed my eyes to see the face of my father. They had been married for nearly 62 years. What was she thinking? What would she do without the man she had spent virtually all of her life with? She sat quietly, steady and patiently waiting for Pop. She sat showing her own strength.

When John Randolph came out to tell us Pop had come through the surgery well, Mom looked at me for confirmation that what the doctor said was correct. "He did great Mom. Dr. Randolph got the cancer, he's gonna make it." Little did we know how tough it would be.

"The most important thing a father can do for his children, is to love their mother."

24 "ICU" – Ignore, Careless & Unconcerned

"Success is a journey not a destination."

- Herman Cain

Pop's recovery was not without incident. Despite the heroic efforts of John Randolph, my father almost didn't make it home from the hospital. Only now do I understand some of the arguments about hospitals. Nurses today don't work for the hospitals; they work for companies that essentially rent them to the hospitals on a daily basis. Thus it's possible, indeed likely, a patient may never have the same nurse two days in a row. For the patient and family this means never establishing a rapport with the very people charged with helping someone heal. It also means more mistakes are likely to occur.

ICU used to stand for intensive care unit. During Pop's recovery, I came to believe it meant IGNORE, CARELESS & UNCONCERNED! From the beginning, it was a comedy of errors, alarms and buzzers going off. A nurse telling me my father was going to have open-heart surgery (while in ICU recovering from the surgery!!!!). Oops, sorry wrong patient! Incorrect medications almost the order of the day and that God awful jargon that hospital employees speak that treats patients as though they are deaf, stupid or already dead.

Patients don't get medicine...they get "meds." The large book of orders and histories, notes and remarks goes almost unnoticed leading to poor to lousy care. When Pop couldn't eat, they put a "peg tube" in his stomach. It was bad enough having it much less to ignore the infection developing around it! When on Christmas day it appeared my father was going to die, I was advised I shou' sign the "DNR"…an order telling them "do not resuscitate" my father if he starts to fail.

We were all at home trying to let life go on as Pop was trying to recover. He had been unconscious for a few weeks and his future was anything but certain. I had gone to the hospital early that morning, stopping by the chapel and asking God to please let Pop live through this most special holiday. Were he to die on Christmas day, no future Christmas would ever again be joyful.

My therapy that day was to return home and prepare dinner for our "family." It was the first holiday "family dinner" at our home that didn't have Pop and I sitting at opposite ends of the table. In our family, the seats at the head of the table are places of honor and respect.

We started dinner with a toast to Pop and wishes of a Merry Christmas, trying our best to enjoy the day. As always, we told stories while enjoying endless courses of food and wine. Around three o'clock the phone rang, and I knew the instant I heard it ring that dinner was over.

It was the hospital calling to tell us we should come down quickly. Patti, the girls, my mother and I flew out the door leaving our guests to finish up. We arrived at the hospital and rushed to Pop's room. Pop was failing. A doctor arrived, not John Randolph, not someone who understood bedside manner, not someone who showed any care or compassion. On the contrary, that Christmas afternoon, the doctor was more like a robot.

I don't know if it was obvious to him that I didn't like him, but it was certainly obvious to everyone in my family. He and I discussed Pop's condition…he was cold, all business, black and white…"your father is dying." I asked if Randolph had seen my father, he mumbled an answer and told me that given the circumstances it would be best if I signed the DNR.

A DNR is effectively a death sentence. You're telling the hospital to let the patient die. It was the worst moment of my life. I felt as though I were executing my father. Someone had to make these decisions and the responsibility had fallen to me. So I signed the order.

I don't remember the exact sequence of events, but we stayed with Pop for a few hours and he appeared to be stable, so we returned home expecting to come back later in the evening. Within a few hours the phone rang, and it was John Randolph ng me he wanted me to rescind the DNR. He let me know in no uncertain terms he completely disagreed with the other physician's decision.

"Give me three days. I'm going to put your father on a respirator and if there is no improvement by then, you can sign the DNR. I told you I'd have your father and you playing golf, and damn it, that's what I'm gonna do."

I had been praying for a miracle and sure enough, my prayers were answered. Randolph told me my father was his patient and he would decide when and if it was time to give up. Sure enough with the aid of the respirator and Randolph's near nonstop care, my father rallied.

Once again, John Randolph had proven himself a determined and extraordinary physician with a heart. My father survived that Christmas day and indeed lived seven more months, As Christmas gifts go, John Randolph and God gave my family and me the best present of our lives.

"Only dead fish swim with the current."

- Oren Harari

25 The Last Vacation

"One of the things my father didn't teach me was how to quit."

- Herman Cain

Over the course of the next few months, my father tried to recover. However, day after day we watched him slowly deteriorate but never give up. When he entered the hospital that first week of December he weighed over 250 pounds. When I took him home in February he was down to less than 180.

Frail, using a walker, unable to eat other than through a tube in his stomach, life for my father was not what we had hoped for. We are Italians. For us life is about family and food. My sister Connie flew in from Florida repeatedly to stay for days at a time to be with our parents. My brother and his family; Russell, the next door neighbor, "third son"; Mike Beighey, one of my managers who wanted Pop to be his father and a host of other people had been coming to the hospital and to Pop's house to pay their respects and show the love and affection on a continuous basis for weeks. All helped us pass the time during those long winter months of recovery.

Over the spring we had moments when it appeared Pop was making headway, only to have those moments dashed by a dose of reality. By late spring, we decided to have yet another specialist look at Pop's throat. Despite the surgery, the cancer had reoccurred making it impossible for him to swallow. Randolph sent us to see Dr. Matthew McBride. On his very first examination, McBride said, "I can fix that." Hours later Pop was able to swallow liquids. In fact, a few days later Pop was swallowing soft whole foods. That weekend Pop attended our daughter, Landi's, high school graduation party and was strong enough for one dance with her.

McBride reopened Pop's throat several more times over the next few months, including the day before we would surprise r parents with a party commemorating their 62rd wedding anniversary. It proved to be the happiest days my parents had in six months. McBride's name was added to our list of guardian angels sent by God to help my father through this storm.

Every year my parents joined my family, my sister and her best friend, Karen, (another surrogate Orza, the 2nd sister) in Cancun Mexico for a week. It was by far some of the most enjoyable times any of us spent. We would eat from morning until night, sit around the pool, eat, laugh, eat, tell stories, eat, walk, eat...life doesn't get any better than that.

Now in the spring of 2000, I made arrangements for what in all likelihood would be our last vacation together. At first we talked about whether or not we should go. By now, Pop was in a hospice program, meaning he probably had less than a year to live. I never told Pop that; in fact, I went out of my way to explain hospice in terms that didn't signal an end. I was confident he knew where he was heading and didn't feel it necessary or beneficial to take away whatever hope he was clinging to.

I spoke with the nurses and doctors about the wisdom of taking Pop to Mexico. Everyone agreed he should go and enjoy himself. They helped arrange for the oxygen tanks he now used to help him breath. They identified a hospital and local doctor, just in case. As the trip approached, Pop seemed to grow stronger.

The day we left, Patti, the girls and I drove over to pick up my mother and him. It was 5 o'clock in the morning, and they were sitting at the kitchen counter, packed and ready to go. The flight down went well. Pop and I played cards for most of the flight. I found myself saying thank you to God for making it easy on Pop. When we arrived, Gary Clark our travel agent had arranged for a limousine to take us to our villa. My folks were impressed and pleased to be riding like big shots in a shiny white stretch Lincoln. In his raspy, whispery voice Pop looked at me and said," What's this?"

"A gift from Gary, Pop...he wanted you to travel in style."

"Nice."

It would be three months before I remembered to thank Gary for that wonderful ride.

We arrived in Cancun on Saturday, July 15, 2000. Over the next two days everything went well. Not our normal week in Cancun but we were all having a good time, and best of all, Pop was able to swallow and eat. About mid day Monday, just after having lunch, Pop started to get up from the table.

"Where you going dad?"

"Lay down."

As I got up to help him, his legs buckled. I got him to his bedroom and he asked me for a blanket. It was probably eighty degrees inside, but he was cold. We let him sleep for a few hours, but when he woke, it was obvious something was wrong.

Too weak to walk, an ambulance took him to the "American Clinic" the hospice personnel had identified. He tried to speak but didn't have the strength. Over the next twenty-four hours, one by one his organs began to shut down. His kidneys struggled to produce urine; lungs couldn't generate enough air to breath. I noticed his fingers turning a blue gray, his hands clammy. He lost consciousness during the night.

I spent the closing hours of Pop's life by his side. I called Oklahoma trying desperately to arrange a plane to fly him home. Some of the last words he spoke to me gave me my mission.

"I don't want to die in Mexico. I want to go home."

"I know Pop. I'll handle it."

And so I called everyone I knew with a plane or access to a plane. Business associates, political friends, anyone and everyone, but to no avail. By Tuesday evening, I realized our only hope would be to charter an air ambulance. Thank God for credit cards because the charter would cost $18,000.

Mid day on Wednesday, a local non air-conditioned ambulance transported Pop and I to the Cancun Airport. The question was would he make it. If so, would he die in flight or at home? On the verge of death with a very weak heart and pulse, I told Pop, "Hang on Dad…we're on our way home. Don't give up Pop. We're going home."

In spite of the overwhelming heat and lack of air conditioning, Pop stabilized. Prior to leaving the hospital, my mother came down with the rest of the family to say goodbye to Pop. I sent everyone back to the hotel to pack for their trip home the next morning. Connie stayed behind to share these final moments with Pop. She and the clinic "doctor" followed the ambulance to the airport. When we arrived at the airport and they were about to load Pop on the plane, I heard Connie say, "I love you dad" and nearly broke down myself.

As we boarded the small jet to fly home to Oklahoma, two men walked up to me and introduced themselves. Paramedics, they said they would be taking care of my father during the flight. "What does he like to be called?" they asked me. I told them, "Everyone calls him 'Pop'." For the next four hours, these two new guardian angels never took their eyes off my father. They monitored his heart rate, pulse, gave him shots, and even though he was unconscious, they spoke to him throughout the flight.

I sat cramped in the corner, my hand on Pop's shoulder, throughout the flight. I kept telling him we were heading home. As we climbed up and out of Cancun, the paramedics told me his heart rate was getting stronger and his pulse had stabilized. Pop was using a storehouse of strength to make the trip home. The two paramedics asked me what I planned to do when we got him to Oklahoma. I said I was taking him straight home.

"Not to the hospital?"

"No." I said. "He's had all the hospitals he needs."

During the flight the two men looked at me and said, "You're doing the right thing taking your father home."

"I know," I said. It was time for him to be in his own bed.

"We live from hope to hope."

- Samuel Johnson

26 Pop Died

"If God did not exist, he would have to be invented."

- Voltaire

As I rode in the ambulance carrying Pop home from the Oklahoma City airport, I looked out the rear window and saw a beautiful, rich orange sunset. The symbolism was almost relaxing; God letting me know my father was passing to the beauty of the after life.

I knew it would be better where Pop was going.

I pulled up to my father's house only to find Russell, Pop's neighbor (the 3rd son). When he saw the ambulance, it was apparent his pain and fear were no less than mine. That night Russell was the first of "Pop's boy's" to come and pay homage to their would-be father. My partner, Jim, and close friend, Mike, followed Russell, all men whose own fathers had died years before...men who had given their love for a father to Pop. Each came to say their final goodbyes. Each had become family to him almost as much as my brother, sister and me.

Watching death conquer someone is a terrible sight. Yet at the same time it's incredible to see the human body's will to live. My father struggled to survive; with each breath his chest would rise and fall trying to win the battle of minutes. I noticed that Pop had developed a death rattle in his chest, as fluids surrounded his heart and filled his lungs, fluids that would eventually kill him.

Over the last several weeks, Pop's arms had become pincushions from the constant flow of shots, IV's and blood samples. He bruised easily, and his arms had grown discolored. He had stopped taking medication to get well. Now it's only purpose was to minimize the pain. As he lay in his own bed, the hospice nurse arrived. She told me he wouldn't need any more medicine. It was time for him to die quietly.

He slept without being disturbed. His eyes were closed but would occasionally open just a hair. I don't know if he could see anything or even if he could hear me, but I spoke to him throughout the night.

"We're home dad. I love you Pop. Thanks for being such a wonderful father. Thanks for being such a terrific husband and grandfather. Thanks for everything you taught me and for everything you did to make sure all of us lived a better life."

The hospice nurse put a warm washcloth on his forehead to comfort him, but I removed it so I could see his face. Over the course of the next seven hours his breathing slowed. Sometimes it would stop for what seemed an eternity only to start again as he cheated death.

When he was in the hospital in Mexico we had removed his false teeth. As I sat there watching him, I realized how hollow his face looked without his teeth. It occurred to me that the man lying in front of me was becoming someone I didn't know or recognize. I found myself staring at the bald spot he had worn in his hair from all the months in the hospital. His hands were thinner, loose with skin that seemed too big for his bones and unresponsive to my grasp.

At midnight, I heard the living room clock strike twelve, thinking to myself that he had made it another day. This was all the more miraculous given the fact we had disconnected his oxygen and IV's hours earlier.

His skin color was now a dull gray, his body growing colder as he lay there. I never stopped holding him. I stroked his silky soft hair and rubbed his hands. He was dying quietly, but not without a fight. He lay in his bed with his digital alarm clock on the nightstand behind him. His death was being documented by the minute as I watched the numbers change on the clock.

About 5:15 a.m. Pop took a long, loud, full gasp of air and stopped breathing. It was almost the sound and feel of a balloon when the air is finally let out. The hospice nurse took his pulse, checked his heart, looked at me and said, "That's it." The numbers on the clock told me the exact moment of death.

I said nothing. I just kept sitting there holding my father in my arms. As she rose to leave the bedroom so I could be alone with Pop, he took another large breath of air. His entire body seemed rise as he filled his lungs with air. I looked at the clock, and it 5:19 a.m.

Pop Died

27 Saying Goodbye

"In three words I can sum up everything I've learned about life. It goes on."

- Robert Frost

The funeral home attendants arrived promptly at 7 a.m. to pick up Pop. As they rolled his gurney to the hearse, they stopped. One of the attendants asked me if I would like Pop's wedding band. I answered yes as they removed it from his hand. I placed it on my left hand next to the ring Patti had given me nearly 20 years before. I have worn both rings since that day.

Pop and the rest of the family had previously decided his body would be cremated, so all that was necessary was to have the body made ready for viewing by the family. Patti, the girls, my sister and mother were flying home from Cancun and scheduled to arrive about noon. I called my brother to let him know the arrangements.

I advised the funeral home we would all come by to say our goodbyes about 1 p.m. Patti landed in Dallas about 10 a.m. that morning and called to check on Pop's condition. Hoping against hope he might have pulled through, she knew the moment I answered that he had died.

In fact, she told me that while on the flight home, my mother had told my sister Connie she knew that her husband of 62 years was gone. While making the final preparations, I began to sort out Pop's belongings. I gave my brother Pop's razor, decided to give his golf clubs to my cousin, one of his golf putters to Mike Beighey, one of Pop's boy's. Later, my sister and I would give away Pop's clothes to various neighbors. Mom would later give me two nail clippers and an old long handled metal shoehorn that Pop kept in his closet. I would also keep a pair of his eyeglasses and his cane. Had these items not been my father's, it would be considered garbage, but because it was his, they were now prized possessions.

I ran a few errands including washing the car. Ironically, at the car wash I ran into Cherokee Ballard, a former news colleague from Channel 5, who was also fighting cancer. She told me her battle was going well. I visited the funeral home to arrange for payment only to have the funeral director tell me how much she enjoyed our Garfield's Restaurant. At a time when I didn't much feel like smiling, I found visiting with Cherokee and the funeral directors comments about our restaurants calming.

The phones at my home, office, Pop's home, the cell phone rang continuously as word passed that my father had died. The calls of condolence were difficult, in fact I was often unable to say anything, my voice cracking as I tried to form words of thanks. Blair Schoeb, a friend who managed my 1990 campaign for governor of Oklahoma, called with poignant comments about how fortunate we were to have such a close knit family. All of these events and many more were cemented in my mind as freeze frames, a sort of photo album of memories other people had and shared with me of my father and family.

Just after noon, my mother, wife, sister and daughters arrived and so did the flowers and plants. Russell came by to share in the loss. I called my brother to tell him we would all meet at the funeral home. With Kleenex and handkerchiefs in hand, we all arrived at 1 p.m. I asked to see Pop first just to ensure that what everyone would see would provide consolation. As I entered the room, there lay Pop. He was covered with a blanket from the neck down, but his face looked great. In fact, it was the best he had looked in weeks. Alone, I spoke with him again, saying goodbye, telling him he looked great and that everyone was here to see him.

I touched his face only to realize it was cold and waxy, not the warm skin I had stroked nearly every day for the last seven months. Slowly, the rest of the family came in to pay their last respects. It was a sea of tears. My mother came in last crying, sobbing, asking why to a question for which there was no answer. She had not really had her chance to say goodbye to Pop in Mexico. He had been unconscious when he and I left the hospital. So now she could only pray he might somehow hear her words of love.

Fifteen or twenty minutes later everyone was gone, and I was alone again with Pop. Now it was time for my final goodbyes...no more Sunday dinners, his seat at the head of the table to someday (not now...not soon) be occupied by someone else. No one commandeering the remote control to switch the channel to the golf tournaments, no more stories of Uncle Eddie, Vic or any of the other brothers and sisters in Pop's family. Never again would I hear that raspy voice telling my mother, wife, daughters how much he loved them...or me "I'm so proud of you."

The next day we had a funeral mass for Pop. My father fought his battle with cancer at a local hospital. Each day a Catholic priest would visit him and give him communion. This little man from Sri Lanka had that wonderful singsong voice common to that part of the world. Pop grew to really enjoy his time with Father Joe. So it was Father Joe I called upon to do Pop's funeral mass. Patti and I went to see him within hours of Pop's death and told him the stories our family shared, gave him a copy of the first edition of this book so he could read about our traditions. As it turned out, Father Joe was the perfect priest to hand over my father's soul to God.

At the mass, the altar was covered in flowers and items reminiscent of his life...his cane, a box of spaghetti, his glasses, a golf club and a dozen or so photographs of Pop and the family, but all that was left of my father was an urn of his ashes. Friends and family notified friends and family. As I stood in the vestibule of the church Friday, July 21st, I was touched by the enormous out pouring of friendship all attending Pop's funeral mass out of respect for him and our family.

Earlier that morning the phone rang at home. It was Kay Mallory, the nurse who had taken such wonderful care of my father after his surgery. She called to ask me if she and her mother could attend Pop's mass. Now as the mass was about to begin, I saw Kay and her mom sitting in a pew.

Over the last eight months, I had managed to oversee my father's illness, surgery, recovery and demise, managed to care for the rest of our family, avoiding as much as possible, occasions of personal pain only to have it all come rushing out at that mass. I cried as I have never cried before, sobbing loudly for the loss I still cannot describe. I had never hurt so badly.

Then and only then did I begin to realize what my wife had been feeling for most of her life. Her father had passed away when she was just seven years old. Decades later she still cried the tears of pain from not having a father. Now, I too understood how painful it is to lose the flesh and blood of your parents.

When the mass was over, I arose and walked to the pulpit taking deep breaths with each step to calm myself. I had one last responsibility to perform in the name of my father. I spoke these words.

"On behalf of my mom and our entire family, Patti and I thank you for being here. Most of you knew Pop. He valued family above everything else in life. To Pop, family didn't always have to be by bloodline.

We often referred to many of you as some of "Pop's boys and girls." And you treated him with love, affection and respect.

To Pop you were family...and with that designation, he didn't shy from telling you what to do with your lives...or how to do it. More important, he was honored when you came to him for advice or direction. I know he would be appreciative of having you here today.

Pop had a lot of simple sayings that helped frame his and our lives. He believed in hard work, competing hard but fairly. He believed in setting a goal and achieving it and in eating because that was the best time to share with family.

Pop always told me the "apple doesn't fall too far from the tree." You know my outlook on life is a mirror of my fathers. I also know that watching him these last few months, I realized I could never match his strength and will to live. Pop never gave up...he fought right until he took his last breath of life.

Pop died at home in his bed. He left behind 83 years of memories and wisdom. These pictures show you some of the many happy moments of Pop's life...most recently, he and Mom celebrating their 62nd wedding anniversary.

I loved my father beyond words. More important, he was never shy about telling me, or any of us, how much he loved us.

Thank you all for sharing these final moments of Pop's life; for your many calls of condolence, the beautiful flowers and for being a part of the many wonderful events you've shared with our family.

Pop loved to eat, and so we invite you to come back to our home for one last celebration of Pop's life. Thank you again for being here and for making Pop's life richer for having known you."

With that, the mass was over and virtually everyone in the church drove home with us for dinner. It couldn't have been nicer. Plenty of food (all Italian)...plenty of wine, much more laughter than tears, endless stories, memories and more friendship than we could ever measure.

The next day I divided Pop's ashes into quarters. I gave my brother and sister theirs and kept a bag for my mother and my family. Ironically, the day of the funeral I received a telephone call from Kathy Tagnesi, the Vice President of Administration at the hospital where Pop had spent so many weeks. She called to tell me she wasn't able to make the funeral because she was just about to leave on a trip overseas. She said, "I have a rather strange request." She told me she understood Pop had been cremated and wanted to know if she could have a small amount of his ashes. Strange indeed, until she told me she was heading to Scotland. She said while she was there, she wanted to make a special trip to St. Andrew's golf course, where she would spread Pop's ashes on the world's oldest and most famous golf course. We both laughed and agreed Pop would get a kick out of that. A few weeks later, she returned home and presented me a variety of gifts all monogrammed with St. Andrew's logo. She also gave me photos of her casting Pop's ashes to the wind at St. Andrews.

Two days after Pop's mass, Connie, my mother, Patti, the girls and I went for a ride to two local golf courses. Slowly we walked to specific tees and greens and spread my father's ashes. I had already spread a few in my front garden. Now whenever I play golf or come home, I say hello to Pop. My father will always be with me. I still wear his ring; have his photo's on my desks at work and home. Believe it or not, despite the long slow death my father endured, there were many moments of laughter and joy. He had a sense of humor, the benefit of family and the natural laughter that comes from the everyday events of life.

A year later, it was time again for the annual family vacation in Cancun. As we had for year's prior, Connie, Karen, Mom, Patti, Alix, Landi and I would spend a week together celebrating family.

It was awkward that first day. We convened for dinner at a local restaurant and after a few moments of normal banter, I raised my glass of wine to toast Pop. All of us clinked our glasses, tears in our eyes and saluted the memory of Pop. For the rest of the evening we enjoyed a warm, funny family dinner, knowing Pop was watching from afar, as we carried on the traditions of our family.

All of this gives meaning to the subtitle of my book... "The Logic, Love And Laughter That Comes From Family".

"If you're feeling low, don't despair. The sun has a sinking spell every night, but it comes back up every morning."

Saying Goodbye

28 An Unexpected Ending...

"Whoever has a heart full of love always has something to give."

- Pope John XXIII

In spite of what I knew to be inevitable, I lied to myself about my parent's mortality. No one lives forever, and as much as I knew my folks would someday be gone, I was never really prepared. Pop's death was slow, painful and depressing and made the entire family die a little as we watched him die. When Mom took seriously ill ten months later and was facing death, we asked God to take her quickly or not at all, but not to let her suffer. He was kind and loving enough to allow us to have her for a while longer. The trouble was, we didn't know how long.

When she recovered and grew stronger and healthier than she had been in years, we all marveled at her resilience. She would drive the three blocks to my office each day and come "to work." Her job was to help with filing, stuffing envelopes and opening the mail. To Mom, it was work on par with finding a cure for cancer, building the space shuttle and designing a skyscraper.

She loved her job. The very fact that she had somewhere to go each day brightened her life. She would awake with purpose, dress for work, put on her make-up, visit the beauty salon to have her hair and nails done, all so she would look professional. She had not had a job for about 40 years; so coming to my office was a big deal.

Her life had changed since Pop had passed away. She had to learn to live alone for the first time in her 87 years of life. She cooked less and when she wasn't eating at our house, she would sit alone and eat dinner at the counter in her home. She sometimes told me the worst part of life without Pop at home was the loneliness. Thus, her job and being with family kept her cheerful and living with purpose. Just prior to Pop becoming ill, their dog died. Thus, the house was made even lonelier without the dog.

On Friday, September 21st Patti, Mom and I left work at 4:30 p.m. to go get Mom a new dog. We had been looking for a small, trained housedog for weeks. Mom was picky. She wanted a certain look, size and breed of dog. That Friday, Patti found what appeared to be the perfect match. A local animal shelter had a website that displayed the dogs they had for adoption. "Tawny" was a four-year old mixed breed that looked like a fox. Mom fell in love with her at first sight. So we drove across town to see Tawny up close. She was living in what the shelter called a foster home. A young couple kept strays rather than having them live in the shelter. We pulled in the driveway about 5:00 p.m. The college girl who lived at the house walked Tawny out to the car. The look on Mom's face was priceless.

We spent about twenty minutes visiting, gave her a check for the dog and loaded Tawny in the car for the trip home. Mom had a new dog! While we were driving, Mom said she had had a dream about Pop the night before.

"I dreamt he was in a crowded room full of people, but I couldn't catch up with him." I thought that strange for a couple of reasons, not the least of which was the fact that she had never mentioned dreaming of Pop before. We all went back to her house to play with the dog. Mom asked us to stay and have dinner with her, which we did. As we were cleaning up and getting ready to leave, Mom told us how pleased she was that we had stayed… "Wasn't this fun?"

Indeed, it had been fun watching her with her new dog. She had a hard time remembering the dog's name. "What's her name?"

"It's Tawny, Mom."

"What?"

"Tawny…you know like Connie (my sister) only with a T."

"Oh…okay."

Later that night she would send Connie an email telling her, she had a new dog. "Its name is Connie!"

The first thing Saturday morning, Patti called Mom to see how she was doing and how the dog had behaved during the night, if she had perhaps wet on the carpet.

"Oh, she was fine. I just came from taking her for a walk."

This was great news since Mom needed to exercise to keep her diabetes in check, so walking the dog helped both of them.

My brother Dan had invited Mom to have dinner with him that evening. Dan's twin daughters were going to celebrate their 14th birthday with Dan and Mom. Patti and I were dressing to go to a movie when the phone rang at 6:30 p.m.

"Vinny...Mom is unconscious. She grabbed her chest saying she had some pain and passed out. I've called an ambulance." As I hung up the phone I found myself thinking, "Please God don't let her suffer."

Patti and I headed for the hospital arriving just minutes after Dan and the ambulance. The moment I entered the emergency room where Mom was laying, I knew it would not be a long evening. Landi was in Nashville at Vanderbilt. Patti called to let her know about Grandma. Alix was with a group of her friends when she received her call from Patti asking her to come to the hospital right away.

The ambulance crew, doctor and nurses were all working feverously trying to save Mom's life. I stood holding Mom, stroking her hair, whispering in her ear, that I was there. Patti and Alix came in to tell Mom they loved her. Dan came in and left. Only a month earlier he had watched his 24-year-old daughter die of complications from Muscular Dystrophy. Our family would lose three Orza's in 24 months. It was a burden worse than any of us had ever imagined.

The rest of the family left the room. I was alone with the doctor, nurses and Mom. Holding her in my arms, I leaned over and told her lifeless body, "I love you Mom. Thank you Mom...thank you for everything. It's okay Mom. Say hello to Pop for me. I love you Mom. I'll miss you Mom. Goodbye Mom."

She had been unconscious since collapsing at Dan's home about 45 minutes earlier. I watched as her heart rate and pulse deteriorated slowly. One of the nurses asked me to step outside, but after being on the wrong side of the curtain for about 4 or 5 minutes, I reentered. I sat holding her, trying to give the doctor and nurse room to work. That's when I realized the nurse was giving Mom artificial respiration. I looked at the monitor and saw her pulse at zero. It was a battle for life that would not be won. I told the doctor they could stop. He did not argue. I sat there as the medical staff began to leave the room. The beeping of the

An Unexpected Ending...   129 monitor stopped when one of the nurses turned it off. I stood and walked from the foot of the gurney to hold Mom in my arms. Crying, it was the second time I had had a parent die in my arms. The tears flooded from my eyes.

Fifty-one years of life somehow changed in a moment. All I could think was that now I had no parents. I asked a nurse to remove the crucifix Mom wore around her neck. Her father had given it to her when she married Pop. A few minutes later, I gave that cross to Alix, the last gift from her grandmother. We removed her wedding band and another ring she had always promised Patti. The next morning when Connie flew in from Florida and Landi came in from Nashville, I gave Connie Mom's wedding band. Patti asked me about giving Landi Mom's other ring. Landi is named after my mother...Landi being Mom's maiden name. I agreed this would be exactly what Mom would have wanted. Landi, Alix and Connie all wear these simple remembrances of Mom.

As I left the emergency room, I looked back one last time at Mom. She lay there still wired to the monitor and a tube in her mouth for the now turned off oxygen. I walked back in for one last goodbye. Her skin had already grown cool to the touch. I hugged her one last time and kissed her goodbye. Before I left the emergency room, I thanked the doctors, nurses and paramedics for all their efforts and help, and then we drove home.

Along the way, I remembered Tawny and so we stopped at Mom's house to let the dog out. The next morning I returned her to the college girl who had been her foster parent. Later that night I climbed into bed and cried again as I had 14 months earlier when Pop died. I knew our family would never be the same without them, but I promised myself I would carry on the traditions of my parents.

The next morning I headed straight for the kitchen to prepare dinner for what was left of our entire family. Later that Sunday afternoon as Mom and Pop had done so many times, we all gathered around the dining room table for our typical Italian dinner. Dan and his family, Connie, Patti, Alix, Landi and I shared the food of heritage, antipasti, macaroni, fruit, pastries, coffee and of course the wine. As we all sat around the table there was a pause, a moment of unplanned silence, and then I lifted my glass and proposed a toast to Mom. Almost in unison, everyone toasted her memory with the simple Italian "salute." Dinner lasted the normal three hours as we all ate, laughed, cried and told stories about our family. I knew Mom and Pop would be proud...the family was together!

SALUTE.

"What the mother sings to the cradle goes all the way to the coffin."
- Henry Ward Beecher

29 Fleas

"A candle loses nothing by lighting another candle."
- Father James Keller *(1900-1977)*
Founder of The Christophers

"Stanislaw Lec wrote, "Thoughts like fleas, jump from man to man. But they don't bite everybody." I sat down to put my thoughts on paper as a result of the many wonderful compliments I received from speaking to groups, schools, businesses and other organizations about what is possible in life. I didn't set out to write a book about family, but rather just to tell stories about life. Hopefully, some of my family 'fleas' bit you! Only as a result of putting my thoughts to paper did I realize how lucky I was to have such wonderful parents and family, fabulous traditions and so many experiences and memories that have made my life better.

My stories are designed to help you think about what has happened in your life. It seems all too many of us want to blame our present on our past but the truth is, we can shape our own lives. If you haven't been lucky enough to have parents, a spouse, children or friends as wonderful as mine, remember there is still time. If you haven't lived out your dreams yet, what are you waiting for? Giving up is wasting the opportunity God gives each of us during our years here on earth. The beauty of life is we can create our future and select the parts of the past we want to remember.

Generally speaking, women do a better job than men in expressing their emotions. It's less common and sometimes unacceptable for men in America to muffle their emotion or affection for each other and that includes our fathers. Sadly, it's often looked upon as a sign of weakness. That means all too many of us allow our fathers, sons and close friends to never hear the simple words of love and admiration we have for each other. If you haven't told your parents, husband, wife or children you love them, do it now, today. I sincerely believe you'll find it to be a cathartic experience that helps heal the wounds of losing someone who has measurably impacted your life...especially if that man was your father. If you don't have goals, make some now, today. In the event things don't go as well as you wish, try again, don't give up.

I still cry about my parents passing, and suspect I will for the rest of my life. Just as I was accepting Pop's death, my mother's sudden death drove me to my knees again. However, life does go on, and thankfully, I have wonderful memories of all the years we spent together. Our daughters are growing up and making us more proud of them each day of their lives. I have become more appreciative and grateful to my friends and family.

No matter how long we live, life is still too short...especially when the life we lose is someone we love. So, when you close this book do yourself a favor. Go find a friend or family member and give them a hug and a kiss and tell them thanks or let them know you love them. Don't ever put it off until another day. God forbid you or they pass on without ever hearing those simple words of thanks and love. Believe me, as much as Patti, Landi, Alix and I miss my parents, we have the satisfaction of not just knowing, but of seeing and hearing how much we all loved each other. Don't waste a moment of whatever time you have on this earth. The logic, love and laughter that comes with family is what makes our time here so meaningful.

By the way, if you give someone a kiss or a hug and they back away or tell you it's not necessary...don't feel shy about telling them...hey..."WHEN I WANT YOUR OPINION, I'LL TELL IT TO YOU."

"To fear love is to fear life...."
- Lord Bertrand A. Russell

Published by *Great Thoughts Books*
1220 South Santa Fe Avenue
Edmond, OK 73003

For large quantities of
"When I Want Your Opinion I'll Tell It To You"
call (405) 705-5055 or e-mail GreatThoughts@eats-inc.com

1 - $10.00 each • 2-10 - $9.25 each • 11-25 copies - $8.50 each
26 or more - $8.00 each

Shipping Charges
1-5 books - $7.95
6-10 books - $9.95
11-25 books - $11.95
26+ books – 8% of order

Order Form			
Qty	Description	Cost Each	Total
	"When I Want Your Opinion, I'll Tell It To You"		
		Shipping & Handling Cost	
		Total Amount Due	

Shipping Address

Name_____

Address _____

_____

City_____ State _____ Zip _____